Prepare for the most exciting experience!

While others are confused by unmanageable debt, declining wages and prices, failing financial institutions, falling real estate prices, and a frantic stock market, you will finally understand how the system truly works.

The opportunities are enormous. During such rapid and massive economic changes, some families will amass tremendous fortunes. Some will pay off all debt, including mortgages. Those who don't know what to do with debt, or which investments will default...will not.

In a writing style you will fully understand, the author rips away the veil of confusion and exposes the stark facts: Of personal, company, and government debt that far exceeds that of 1929. How governments cannot create wealth, but only influence its transfer between individuals.

It's time for you to be on the receiving side. During perhaps the most rapid and massive transfer of wealth ever experienced.

You will learn how to do this not from a politician or seller of securities, who have obvious vested interests, but from an independent investment adviser and futurist, whose clients avoided the stock market crash of 1987 and the rapid fall in gold investments in 1980.

Determine immediately what is happening and why. What you can do about it, regardless of your current financial situation.

For it is the Year of Jubilee...

*DEBT-FREE
   IN FOUR YEARS...*

There are only two or three human stories,
and they go on repeating themselves as fiercely
as if they had never happened before.
—Willa Cather

DEBT-FREE IN FOUR YEARS...

Robert E. Strayer

Barclay House
New York

A BARCLAY TRADE PAPERBACK
Published by: Barclay House
A division of the Zinn Publishing Group
ZINN COMMUNICATIONS / NEW YORK

Copyright © 1995 by Zinn Communications

All rights reserved. No part of this book may be reproduced or transmitted in any form or by any means, electronic or mechanical, including photocopying, recording , or by any information storage and retrieval system, without the written permission of the Publisher, except where permitted by law.

ISBN: 0-935016-33-3

Printed in the United States of America

Library of Congress Cataloging-in-Publication Data

Strayer, Robert E., 1945–
    Debt Free In 4 Years : eliminate finance burden in your life forever / Robert E. Strayer.
      p.   cm
    Includes Index
    ISBN 0-935016-33-3 (pbk. : alk. paper)
      1. Finance, Personal.   2. Debt.   3. Saving and Investment.
I. Title.
HG179, S8455   1995
332.024'02–dc20   95-43020
                                        CIP

Attention computer users: This book is also available electronically, and is the first in a concept called "The Living Book." Readers are encouraged to challenge and debate stated concepts, ask serious questions, offer further supporting evidence, and provide confirming examples to the author, to further refine subsequent electronic versions for the benefit of all future readers and investment students. Readers are invited to call, via modem, an online service for total interaction at (916) 962-3467. (The remainder of Strayer's trilogy on Financial Serenity, Self-Development, and Spiritual Growth is immediately available electronically, via this online service.)

To my loving father, Virgil,
for the wisdom to look with open eyes;
the courage to risk;
the warmth to share;
the freedom to cry tears of joy.

Contents

EDITOR'S NOTE	XIII

PART ONE: THE PROBLEM

Denial	3
Dysfunctional Families	4
Dysfunctional Companies	5
Dysfunctional Countries	9
Our Dysfunctional Relationship to Money	12
The "Setup"	14

PART TWO: THE SOLUTION

1. **Our Belief Systems**	27
Sources of Financial Information	28
What Everyone Knows Isn't Worth Knowing	36
2. **The Facts Revealed**	41
Inflation and Deflation Explained	43
The Fed Factor	48
The Powerless Federal Reserve Board	50
Adjusting for Inflation	52
Myths About Inflation	56
Summary	57
3. **The Harmony of Business Cycles**	59
The Deflation Cycle (54-Year)	60
The Recession Cycle (7-Year)	74
Causes of Deflation and Recession Cycles	78

4.	**Evaluation**	**85**
	Balance Sheet	86
	Income and Expenses	93
	Spending Review	100
	Evaluation of All Investments	103
5.	**Better Choices**	**119**
	Choices-Target Budget	120
	Found Money Tips	128
6.	**Focus and Courage**	**133**
	Common Stocks	135
	Treasury Bonds	140
	Gold Mining Stocks	148
	Real Estate	155
	Options	162
	No-Load Mutual Funds	166
	Money Market Funds	168
7.	**Your New Strategy**	**171**
	The Big Picture	172
	When To Buy and Sell	181
	Stock Indicators	185
	The Sentinel Index	187
	Bond Indicators	188
	Gold Mining Stock Indicators	189
	Mutual Fund Families	190
	Summary	194
8.	**Financial Planning**	**197**
	Goal-Setting	197
	Financial Serenity	200
	Financially Vulnerable	201
	Shelter-Secure	202
	Debt-Free	202
	Financial Security	203
	Summary	205

❖ *Table of Contents* ❖

9.	**Financial Freedom**	**209**
	Your Road Map	212
	Decide On Professional Assistance	212
	Reposition Investments	213
	Starting Your Conventional Account	221
	Conventional Account Investing	222
	Starting Your Superfund	223
	Superfund Investing	224
	IRA Investing	224
	New Found Money	226
10.	**Vigilance and More Growth**	**227**
	Increasing Income (Employees)	228
	Increasing Income (Self-Employed)	234
	Vigilance of Your New Strategy	235
11.	**Financial Seeking**	**241**
12.	**Financial Sharing**	**245**
	GLOSSARY OF TERMS	251
	APPENDIX	261
	INDEX	263
	AUTHOR'S BIOGRAPHY	269

Editor's Note

THE AUTHOR STRESSES a major secret to successful saving and investment: Accurately predicting the future. Strayer proved this in 1987, when he became one of only a handful of investment advisers nationwide to move his clients totally out of common stocks, avoiding a 35% decline in two weeks.

As one single source to both novice and professional investor, this book will provide answers to questions about money that have plagued you for years. Why is money the greatest source of conflict within families? Why do Americans find it so difficult to save? Why does a market plummet after everyone has decided it's the perfect investment that will never fall in price? How do the economy and investments really work, and how are they related to debt? Why do individuals buy investments they don't totally understand...from institutions that operate in unknown ways?

In brief, we receive little to no training in this extremely important area of our lives. Who learns budgeting at an early age? Who, regardless of his "wealth," does not worry about money? How does one deal with greed?

It is the absence of vested interests that has allowed the author to see what most others do not. As an independent adviser, he has always refused to accept commissions on the investments he recommends, and always declines custody of client funds. These rare policies also prevent misappropriation of funds or the recommendation of inappropriate investments sold only for the commission.

Strayer is ultimately qualified to write such a book. A futurist and President of his own investment advisory firm, he provides marvelous insight to the cycles that affect *all* developments. Graduate work taught him how to research. Two degrees in the sciences provided the training to assimilate the complex and apparently unrelated. His twelve years' management experience with a huge multinational corporation taught him capitalism at its best. Twenty years of successful investment experience taught him not only the rules of investing, but the exceptions. Living and working overseas six years as a consultant provided a world view of how everything fits together. Personal and spiritual work helped him glimpse the All. And many years in Toastmasters International honed his ability to express the complex in a very understandable fashion.

Strayer is an ideal teacher of saving and the mastery of financial investments. He has counseled numerous average individuals on money management. He has also served as an adviser to stockbrokers, bankers, financial planners, CPAs, business owners, economists, and even Nobel prize-winners. You can also now benefit from "the experts' expert."

His technical research reveals an overall harmony to everything. Cycles and patterns massively influence economic, health, and social developments *at the same time*. You too will see how these trends work, where we are in each, what to expect, and what to do about it. But whether it be financial debt or psychological debt (expectations), he goes on to identify generic debt as the key source of all chaos. Furthermore, debt of all types ebbs and flows in very predictable cycles of 7 and 50/60 year periods.

The personal and the financial cannot be totally separated. As a result, Strayer presents this financial education and strategy in what is called the Twelve-Step format. He believes this approach is not only a way of life anyone can benefit from, but an ideal approach for teaching anything.

It is now obvious that the symptoms of financial and economic insanity are inflation and debt. Inflation is certainly present, and the purchasing value of the dollar has plummeted 79% in the last three decades via inflation. Personal, business, and government debt has skyrocketed to unprecedented levels, even surpassing that of 1929.

This book peels back the veil of illusion disguising the insanity of our current financial and economic problems, laying them bare. It then provides a timeless solution to prosperity, enabling anyone to become totally debt-free by 1998.

The author also shares the many ways others have erred, or invested inappropriately, sometimes with disastrous results. Because of this, he has always expressed gratitude to clients who shared past negative experiences, which in most cases was the reason they came to him for assistance. Understanding their errors will hopefully help you avoid making the same mistakes.

Despite the quantum changes of all types now facing our nation, we are already moving in a more conservative and gentle direction. Most changes will be welcomed. But the withdrawal pains from debt addiction will be extremely painful to those who do not understand what is happening.

It is now time to finalize your mastery of money...for it is, as Strayer describes in Chapter Three, The Year of Jubilee.

The Editor
1995

Part One

THE PROBLEM

Denial

*A problem must be recognized,
before it can be solved.*

EVERYTHING RELATED TO investing is simply the result of what most people are thinking at any point in time. In other words, financial developments are only symptoms of this collective thinking.

During certain periods of time, society is caring and giving, and self-esteem runs high. This will be reflected by healthy economic conditions and conservative, rational, and healthy finances among individuals. During other periods, society is largely dysfunctional and self-esteem runs low. This will be reflected by volatile, dysfunctional economic conditions as well as greed, a sense of lack, materialism, speculation, and high levels of debt among individuals. In other words, society directly affects how much most people earn, spend, save, and owe.

To become, or remain, financially successful, we must therefore gain a new respect for such "mob psychology." This explains how all investments move into and out of favor, as well as how companies and even entire countries ebb and flow between sanity and insanity.

You might be shocked to learn that incredibly powerful cycles influence financial, health, and social trends *at the same time*. But these long-term cycles are also extremely predictable, as will be explained in Chapter Three. Once you understand how cycles function, you will hold the key to massively improving your finances, or avoiding incredible losses. You will no longer react to change, but actually be able to *anticipate* major developments.

If you so desire, such understanding can also be used for even greater benefit: Increased self-awareness and even spiritual growth. The grand puzzle does fit together, and nothing is random.

We will begin by briefly looking at the current level of well-being or dysfunction within families and society. This will provide enormous insight as to where we are in business and financial trends. Because they are one and the same.

Dysfunctional Families

It is estimated that as much as 96% of our population is currently dysfunctional (Gravitz and Bowden, *Recovery: A Guide for Adult Children of Alcoholics*). Most of us are currently at a cyclical low point of emotional health. Dealing with this problem, however, is the subject of another entire book now being completed. Even though this book is presented in the Twelve-Step format, it only indirectly deals with financial lack, fear, and greed, without attacking the root cause. It was necessary to publish everything related to the financial early due to massive, impending economic change.

But even if the causes of low self-esteem are not immediately apparent, the symptoms are quite obvious. They include alcohol and other drug abuse, chronic worry, rage, violence, overly-rigid parental attitudes, perfectionism, apathy, depression, emotional abuse, sexual abuse, physical abuse, workaholism, abandonment, missing children, the homeless situation, fear, frustration, and loneliness.

Unfortunately, most of us are in massive denial of such problems. In other words, we don't even recognize how sad the overall situation has become.

The scorecard is truly frightening. John Bradshaw, *Bradshaw On: The Family*, points out that sixty million Americans

❖ *Denial* ❖

are seriously affected by alcoholism, 50% are overweight, thirty-four million adult women were sexually abused by age 13, ten million people are victims of violence in families every year, 9 of 10 men and scores of women have extramarital affairs, and half of our marriages end in divorce. Children run away from home to escape mental or physical abuse; sleeping disorders are common; we're addicted to television and prescription drugs; and workaholism is rampant. Alcohol and other drug abuse is epidemic. We are killing ourselves with stress.

The individual is not the only person affected. Within such a complex society we influence many other people every day in an unkindly manner. Our behaviors are also passed from generation to generation. It is not unusual in therapy to see patterns maintained for five generations within a family. Furthermore, during an age of virtually instantaneous communications, our ideas and thoughts are quickly transmitted to others. We are constantly bombarded with confusing messages from the press, television, and our leaders at all levels. So any sanity or insanity spreads with a speed unknown in history, thanks to a virtual exponential explosion of communications technology.

Unfortunately, most such communication is still negative. Guilt, blame, and shame are the norm. It is obvious this is the age of the dysfunctional family.

Dysfunctional Companies

The concept of dysfunctional families can be extended to business families. This is an important concept, because companies and organizations provide our incomes and place food on our tables. Several years ago, *The Peter Principle* became a best seller. The author was trying to explain why most companies simply don't work. The basic answer was "people move higher in organizational responsibilities until they reach their own level of incompetence." I beg to differ. Businesses aren't working because 96% of the people involved, from owner to employee, are experiencing personal problems.

Take, for example, the dysfunctional individual who's fraught with greed and has decided to make his first million on his own. Or perhaps that same person couldn't get along with superiors or always knew "a better way." He starts his own business. Let's assume the new enterprise somehow avoids those 90% of new businesses which fail, and actually makes money. Because the owner (the business family "parent") is dysfunctional, the business family will be dysfunctional. If an employee is largely functional, he will soon leave, even if he has to unconsciously pick a fight to justify departure. He simply doesn't fit, and knows it. If employees are dysfunctional, which is typical, there might be a "match."

Dysfunctional companies are easy to recognize. The emphasis is on sales, rather than service and the customer. Employees are not driven by the will to perform out of giving, but by fear. Basic, open, written management reviews are nonexistent. Feelings and ideas move downward in the organization, not up. Dissatisfaction is shared between employees and not with superiors. Inconsistency is the norm, not predictability. Eventually dysfunction will show up in earnings.

There are countless different types of dysfunctional families, involving emotional abuse, perfectionism, manipulation, rage, guilt, abandonment, etc. Having served as a business consultant, I have personally witnessed every single family dysfunction in business families except for physical abuse. Although less prevalent, there are several such cases described in the press. I've even observed incest: The owner, "the parent," has an affair with an employee, "the child," with one or both being married.

Abandonment issues are epidemic in small companies. The employee has received no written management reviews listing strengths and competencies he can show to the next potential employer. The worker simply sits on pincushions at his current job, waiting in fear for the proverbial walking papers. Question: Is this any different from being in your third foster home as a child? Following a dismissal, the fear can be

❖ *Denial* ❖

tremendous. Have you ever looked for a job as an unemployed person? The potential employer is virtually always preoccupied with why the individual was fired from or left his previous job.

But there is one important difference between dysfunctional families and dysfunctional businesses. When born into the family, one enters in relative innocence. When entering a business family as an adult, one is already dysfunctional. It is not surprising that businesses have such problems. It is surprising they can often muddle through as long as they do in spite of it.

But we can't place full blame on this type of family "parent." Particularly with businesses, the employee must also shoulder part of the responsibility. This is most obvious in the worker who feels society owes him a living. This viewpoint is most popular among the most incompetent and unreliable. After all, the owners have the right to receive profits from their commitment of time and money. Should workers have the right to demand higher wages when the company starts losing money? Certainly not. Something has to give. Unfortunately, companies are frequently forced to let people go, when all could potentially keep their jobs, each sharing part of a wage reduction. (Current benefits arrangements, however, help prevent such logical approaches.) This does not release company management from being fair and reasonable, but management-labor problems are legend. If only both could simply recognize they're a team, trying to win for the benefit of all. But this is rare.

Major corporations have a particular cross to bear. When company size reaches the tens of thousands, bureaucracies are created. Functional companies of this size exist, but are extremely rare. I worked twelve years in management for a major corporation this is often referred to as one of the best-managed companies in America. I'm not sure if that was true. Perhaps their supertanker was simply headed in the same direction as economic flow during the 1970s. But an amazing number of things worked. Caterpillar, Inc. had the most envied international distribution system in the world. The company was a classic "Management by Objectives, Evaluation By Results" corporation. Yearly objectives for each individual were written and agreed to. It was known when an assignment was to be accomplished, and goals were challenging but attainable. How each objective was realized was the responsibility of the person assigned the project.

Each employee was provided an annual written management review. Before the review, both supervisor and employee would complete a form. Five areas were evaluated with a numerical value assigned to each. When added, a perfect score was 100. It was unusual if the two valuations differed by more than 3 to 5 points. During the oral review the employee freely shared areas in which he could improve and could request additional training. He also presented what he felt were his strengths, personal objectives that would benefit his work, and his ambitions within the company. If significant problems existed, potential remedies were discussed. The supervisor then summarized the evaluation and the employee was provided a copy. The important point here is that everyone knew where he stood. And everyone could prove on paper his performance with the company. This was valuable for future job applications.

Rules and procedures automatically grow as companies increase in size. This is how bureaucracies develop. But even with a huge company of Caterpillar's size, there was still flexibility. For example, there were several occasions when a special situation seemed to be at odds with major policy. I was never turned down when I requested variances to such policy. I'm not suggesting Caterpillar was a totally functional company. Supervisors were not equally evaluated by the employee during reviews. I also found to my amazement that one manager immediately below the post of Vice-President didn't understand the true cause of inflation. Although the company spent untold millions on training, economic education was not conducted. This was perhaps proved in the early 1980s when major worldwide economic winds changed direction, catching

❖ *Denial* ❖

the company totally off guard. But as a management model for huge companies, Caterpillar qualifies.

Size appears to be a critical consideration. Tom Peters, the reigning "guru" of American business, found at least one very functional company who believes work and plant units should never exceed two hundred people. Above that number depersonalization occurs, which sharply decreases efficiency. Another critical factor seems to be shared ownership. When the employee owns a part of the company, he or she has a vested interest in assuring that all goes well. Ideas for improvement are shared immediately, particularly if related bonuses are available. Employees feel more at home in their work surroundings, teamwork is very obvious, and people simply work very hard. But this seems only to apply to smaller organizations. Simply because an employee owns shares in his huge corporation does little. The perceived value of individual effort is lost because of size considerations.

I do not profess to be a professional analyst or theoretician on business practices. But I am trying to make one very important point. Small businesses and large companies are families too. We have the parents (owners and managers) and also the children (employees). And with such a huge percentage of the population dysfunctional, it is as hard, if not more difficult, to find a functional business family as it is to find a functional family.

Dysfunctional Countries

If we can extend the concept of dysfunctionality from families to businesses, it is natural to look at entire countries. This too is important, because government actions affect us more than ever before. Here we find more of the same.

The United States, for example, is the critical parent of the world. The messages are very clear: "Don't do as I do, do as I say." "I know, you don't know." "If you need help, always ask me." As a result, our country has overextended its attempted control to the point of futility.

Often this is done in the name of military defense. We've ended up paying the defense bills for numerous other countries. Some of these nations are even starting to object to our missiles being present within their borders, or our warships harboring in their ports. The best and only way to teach is by example. Coercion will always fail.

This stance might sound isolationist. But we must come to accept what we can control and what we must let go. We only have control over ourselves, and even this has become questionable over the past several years. And as long as we keep trying to "fix" other countries, we will avoid looking at ourselves.

One of the best examples is Africa. America has found itself on the wrong side of virtually every major change on that continent over the last thirty years. One exception was Egypt. And how did reasonable relations with that country develop? By letting it go. Egypt finally turned to the Soviets and received a good close look at what that meant. The result was the throwing out of all such influences and finally turning back to the West. To this day, every cheap, flimsy product in that country is called Russian.

Such control issues can be compared with trying to change the behavior of an alcoholic. We can rant, rave, and create enormous guilt in the individual, but time after time only the simplest solution works. This is to explain to the person that we can't agree with his choice; we will no longer accept the chaos. We provide him with tools on how to get help. We then shut up and let him go. When no longer pressured for change, the individual will eventually choose for himself what he really wants. Very often it is only by this approach that change results, if any change will ever occur.

Why are we so insistent on trying to force our political and social values on other countries? Do we want them to become just like us? And what does that mean? As a citizen of another country I'm not sure I would enjoy such a society: A 50% divorce rate, one of the lowest savings rates in the world, rampant alcohol and other drug abuse, huge numbers of home-

❖ *Denial* ❖

less, the highest crime rate in the Western world, and the dubious honor of being the world's largest debtor country.

One good way to identify a dysfunctional family is how rarely the "parents" say "I was wrong." How often have we heard a politician admit to error? Does this mean all past laws and decisions were appropriate? No. Our leaders simply haven't developed the humility to admit error. And until they do, old useless and expensive legislation and appropriations will never be reviewed. We will simply continue to try to patch and throw more money at the results of mistaken past decisions.

We love our democracy, but with our millions of laws telling us what we can and cannot do, how free are we? Thomas Jefferson would twist in his grave. At this point, some might respond "If you don't like it, why don't you leave?" This is the standard parent-child message found in any dysfunctional family or business. It's because I love this country so much that I weep at the slow but steady disintegration. Until we quit trying to fix other countries and concentrate on cleaning up our own mess, nothing will change. And trying to change behavior and symptoms at the *behavioral* level will never work. We can throw as many guns into other countries as we want, and waste billions on "Just Say No" efforts to fix our drug problem, and nothing will change. Perhaps the next major program, as one comedian suggests, is attacking the homeless problem with the phrase "Just Get A House."

We must concentrate on the *true* cause to make a difference. Just as the alcoholic must hit his bottom and decide it simply doesn't work anymore, we must likely do the same as a country. But as will be discussed later, another scenario is unfolding that will hasten a return to sanity. One purpose of this book is to describe this dramatic process and prepare you for the unfathomable change that will result.

This is how denial works, and the results of that process. Whether it be personally, or within a family, company, or country, no change is possible until we peel back the veil and take a close look at the situation at hand. But review is impossible as long as we stay within ourselves or in the situation. For example, the only way I could tell the United States was in such sad financial shape was by living outside the country and comparing that nation with others.

This is similar to a computer that only makes one mistake, that $1 + 1 = 3$. Can you imagine the errors it would create? And that computer can self-analyze itself forever, and not see anything is wrong. But by comparing results with other units, at least the existence of a problem can be recognized. The solution, however, cannot be resolved at the end result of its calculations, because these are only symptoms. To correct the problem, one must determine what is true.

Denial is broken when we move from "I don't know that I don't know" to "I finally realize I really didn't know. That it's simply not working." Only then can real progress start, on a personal basis, within our company families, and with our national family. And the only place to start is with "I."

Our Dysfunctional Relationship to Money

With a better understanding of dysfunctionality in general, it's time to confront the most common: Our relationship to money. One saying in Twelve-Step circles is "You're as sick as your secrets." This is more true for money than for any other difficulty. People will share their sexual problems with another before they will discuss their financial situations or money problems.

This is because we have been taught our financial success is an important measure of our self-worth. But the problem is even more complex. Who is more "worthy"...the rich man who frantically seeks more, or the poor man who agonizes daily with near-poverty?

Both are sick, and both are probably in denial. As a professional investment adviser for fifteen years, and a successful investor for even longer, I've found that one's financial serenity is primarily dependent on the level of personal self-esteem. Income is seldom a good measure of happiness. In fact, in-

❖ *Denial* ❖

come has virtually nothing to do with it. I've counseled people who earned $70,000 a year who simply couldn't save, were laden with debt, and were very unhappy. I've also worked with couples, both employed but making only $25,000 between them, who were financially content and had a savings and investment program.

Early in my financial consulting career, I was perplexed by two common problems: Why did so many people have financial problems? And secondly, why were those with money so reluctant to adopt a more sensible investment approach? I now know the answers to both: Dysfunctional belief systems and denial.

Although finances are not a measure of self-worth, they are often a reliable indicator of more serious personal problems. After years of Twelve-Step work, and now as a sponsor or counselor to others following that path, I've found that a great percentage of people in such programs have money problems. Because finances are so often considered a measure of self-worth, those with money often will not turn to Twelve-Step programs...basically saying "See, I'm not sick." But because such programs still represent a typical slice of Americana, many program people also have good incomes and savings. In such cases, greed is often an issue, or perhaps the individual also attends Debtors Anonymous. But even average investors will see in Chapter Three that economic, social, and health cycles move in tandem. When the economy starts searching for its "bottom" like the alcoholic, *methods for making money and investing will suddenly be reversed*. The techniques one has successfully used in the past, particularly those involving debt, suddenly turn on us and negatively affect our financial health. In fact, we will see that *debt* is the key to this entire book. Whether it be financial debt or psychological debt (expectations).

Very few people approach what could be described as financial serenity. You would be amazed at what I've observed as a professional investment adviser over the last fifteen years.

I've found that people tend to fall into one of two categories. The first group, by far the minority, would be considered rich by most standards. Their "net worth" is high, but are they happy? The answer is generally no. As in any dysfunctional relationship, there is never enough. This individual has progressed from lack to greed. How much is enough? The answer is always "just a little bit more." Similar to the alcoholic, one drink might be too much but ten are never enough. Or greed might shift to fear of losing what one has.

When one reviews the balance sheets of supposedly rich people, one common denominator is virtually always present. This is debt. Donald Trump is a prime example. In fact, debt was an important part of most strategies for becoming wealthy. If you buy anything with 10% down and borrow the rest, two advantages are gained. You can pay back the debt in cheaper dollars as inflation reduces the value of each dollar. Secondly, if the price rises for any reason (and the cause is generally inflation), the return on your investment increases dramatically. But these two advantages violently turn on you if and when prices drop, or the debt load becomes unmanageable. More on this later.

The second monetary category is lack, or fear of loss of income. This is where you will find three of every four adult Americans. More than 70% of households have no money left over at the end of the month. When sharing this statistic with most people, their financial worries lessen. "I have that much company?" It's like walking into an AA meeting and running into both your neighbors, your spouse, and all your kids. This realization doesn't fix the problem, but there is strength in numbers. It also makes it easier to share one's money problems. And until we admit such problems to ourselves and another, perhaps a professional, denial will likely remain.

The "Setup"

The average American simply increases his spending to match his income. Period. This is a sad fact, but true. Regardless of whether income increases by hard work, a bonus, a

❖ *Denial* ❖

salary increase, or inflation, spending simply rises to meet that new level. Americans are among the poorest savers in the world, and generally have little to no reserves on hand for inevitable emergencies. This would not be so bad if spending were only for miscellaneous items that could be quickly eliminated if and when income declines. Instead, virtually all financial problems start in the same way, with monthly debt obligations.

Let's consider an example. Even young people typically buy a house as soon as possible. One or two cars are bought on monthly installments. Credit card debt rises to create a certain minimum monthly payment. It's not unusual to see the following:

$ 800	Monthly Mortgage Payment
$ 350	Car Payments
$ 300	Credit Card Minimum Payments
$1450	Total Monthly Debt Payments

Add to this all the other very necessary monthly expenses like food, clothing, utilities, insurance, etc. and we arrive at a total that is quite intractable. For the majority of Americans this is equal to income...we simply must come up with the total every month, come hell or high water. It is this stark fact that creates daily fear in our lives. Unconsciously we wonder if something could happen to prevent us from paying those monthly bills. We also ponder the humiliation of not meeting these obligations we've created for ourselves, consciously or unconsciously.

It doesn't take much for these fears to be realized. This is particularly true today, with so many jobs being eliminated. With no reserves, all it takes is a forced decrease in salary or wages, which is becoming increasingly common. In most households, both spouses now work to meet obligations. If he or she is laid off, the result is serious problems. There are many other realities like divorce, an extended illness, an unexpected large bill...anything can imbalance the situation. If and when one of these events occur, the result is something called high anxiety. This is *The Setup*.

Why do we get ourselves into such tenuous predicaments? First, most Americans are now addicted to materialism. When we want something we must have it now. We'll worry about paying for it later. We end up mortgaging our income many years into the future.

Secondly, we accumulate tons of various types of debt because of U.S. tax laws. We could write off the interest! Even our CPA often suggests we finance a major purchase for tax purposes instead of paying cash. In 1986 a change in tax laws made this advantage less attractive, but our habits are well-established and difficult to break. But even today, the United States has the most debt-induced tax laws in the world. With such enormous incentives to borrow, why should we even think about saving?

The third reason is because of something called inflation. The rules are firmly ingrained in our minds: "Borrow money and pay it off in cheaper dollars." And, "Inflation will force income higher, making it easier to pay off our debt."

My friend, every 50 to 60 years, as we'll see later, inflation turns into something called deflation. The economy slows dramatically and the dollar becomes more valuable instead of less valuable. We are now entering such a period. Now that we've been "set up," a sharply declining economy and deflation will decrease wages, and monthly debt payments will become more and more difficult to pay off, instead of easier.

So *debt* is the underlying problem. When income drops, debt payments remain the same and must be serviced. Debt levels are far beyond record highs of the past, and we're now in the stratosphere. We have become a nation of credit junkies, and our withdrawal pains from debt will cause high anxiety not seen since "The First Grapes of Wrath."

We've already compared families to companies in several ways. But small companies and major corporations have set themselves up in the same way as described above. The cost

❖ *Denial* ❖

of servicing debt, as a percentage of profits, has increased sharply in the last thirty years for companies. This makes U.S. corporations particularly vulnerable, in the event of any new economic downturn. Companies entered the exhaust phase of increased debt in the 1980s, and the piper must now be paid.

Although rare, a few companies have accumulated cash hordes. What usually happens? A debt-laden company, often smaller, performs a hostile takeover with junk bonds and other debt to access those riches. Often these rare critters accumulate debt to make themselves less palatable. This is akin to an animal in a trap chewing off its foot to escape. Insanity is reigning over Wall Street and Main Street. The first phase of the collapse in low-grade bond prices in 1989 was only one of many harbingers of the coming deflation.

The federal government has also fallen into this same setup. With one difference. Those trusted people in Washington who might be expected to safeguard our monetary system are the biggest abusers of all. They don't even have to balance their budget! Massive and chronic yearly budget deficits since the 1960s have produced a debt pyramid that is quivering and quaking at this very moment. The Savings and Loan crisis was only the first straw. Massive bank failures are lurking just around the corner. The national debt is now approaching five trillion dollars! That's about $33,000 for every taxpayer in the country. The granary is empty and the basement is full of IOUs.

But Poor Uncle is still trying to shore up every major weak industry in the country. This is literally "enabling" at its worst (postponing the recipient's day of reckoning). Companies large and small should be allowed to fail as well as prosper. This is how capitalism works, if we truly believe in that system. If your products or services aren't wanted, or the organization is sick, money should flow to deserving companies via the free market. There was great debate and consternation over whether Sam should spend $1.5 billion to bail out Chrysler more than a decade ago. But today they are spending hundreds of times that amount to "fix" savings and loans.

And there could be heard hardly a whimper in Congress or from taxpayers. Has your voice been heard? What will happen when the banks follow suit? Where will your money be when the quiche hits the fan? Our economic situation will be turned upside down when the greatest debt addict in the country hits his bottom. And what happens to government revenue during a deflation? What would you guess happens to tax revenues during a sharp economic slowdown? Particularly when taxes on illusionary inflation gains suddenly disappear.

Debt is eating this country alive, from every direction imaginable. And inflation has been destroying the value of our currency for decades. These things shall pass, but not without severe pain for those who owe others money.

This is not a crackpot view of the situation. Shortly after the first crash of stocks in 1987, the following comments appeared in *The Sacramento Bee*. The author was H. Ross Perot. Some might not agree with his viewpoints, but he stated the problem very well:

> "...The new turmoil on Wall Street brought home to all of us how serious our economic problems are... The first thing we have to do is stop telling ourselves that everything is all right, and that all the fundamentals are sound. Such statements ignore the obvious. A person with a drinking problem must admit that he is an alcoholic before he can be cured."
>
> "...We Americans have evolved from a tough, resilient people, willing to sacrifice for future generations, into a people who want to feel good now at any price and let the future take care of itself. Put more directly, we have become credit junkies, shooting up huge sums of borrowed money on a government and personal level looking for a new high..."

❖ *Denial* ❖

The same dire concerns are also expressed by those deep inside the government, when they finally leave those posts and are free to speak their minds. John Exter, former Vice-President of The New York Federal Reserve Bank, said the following in 1978:

> "The problems of our international monetary system today are horrendous, indescribable, even incomprehensible. They have been caused by excessive running of the paper money printing presses by all central banks, more by some than by others. Such excesses will inevitably bring their punishment, economic contraction."

Of course the situation is significantly worse today, following the "debt decade of the 80s." And as any professional investor can tell you, major shocks occur when everyone becomes complacent about a situation.

It is nevertheless difficult to find knowledgeable people who don't have a vested interest in what is said. Ravi Batra is one of the top theorists on trade in the world. A Professor of Economics at SMU, he wrote *The Great Depression of 1990*. Mr. Batra has done some wonderful cycle research, and believes we are on the verge of a great downturn in the economy. Other than on a cyclical basis, he believes we top out economically when the most money finds its way into the fewest hands. He also correlates that peak with a time in which the most economic laws are passed.

The latter two items make sense. When money is widely distributed, the ripples or waves are smaller. That is, one problem does not a crisis make. But our total economic system is now at the mercy of financial mistakes made by the few, who also assume greater risks. The world's largest real estate developer, Olympia & York, who is still experiencing major problems, is a prime example. And how much money and control are now in the hands of those few members of Congress? And how have they been doing? We once disputed the concept of government in Russia, particularly socially and economically, because it was centrally-controlled. How free have we truly become? Do citizens or does Washington truly control America? Incidentally, if the most money is in the hands of true saints, we can achieve grandeur. But if in the hands of greedy, power-hungry people, the result is eventual chaos.

In terms of laws passed, when we work ourselves into a very tenuous situation we pass numerous laws to "patch" and "fix" the situation. Judgment, in general, increases as we also try to make others guilty. Millions of laws also make the system more brittle. With fewer laws the system is more dynamic and flexible, more self-adjusting, preventing major shocks.

In terms of the amount of money and who controls it, and the proliferation of new and existing laws, we are now "there." I agree with Mr. Batra's analysis of an epic economic downturn starting in 1990, although the ways in which we arrived at the same conclusion differ somewhat. In exactly January of 1990, the stock market of the world's major economic engine (Japan) began its meltdown, and California real estate began a long decline. More on this later...

But we must admit that a major cause of our current problems lies with us, the people. We have, in the strictest sense, abdicated massive responsibilities to government. We don't want to mess with it. "They'll fix it." Most Americans don't even vote anymore! We are responsible for the destruction of our monetary system and an economic situation that is now at critical mass.

The hallowed halls of Congress are much too far from the people, except in the case of vested interest groups. One simply cannot govern such an enormous country from Capitol Hill. We must move most major decisions to local governments, as far down as city levels when possible. We also need *statesmen* in office, who focus on the best interests of all the people, rather than politicians.

The federal government has reached such a state of finan-

❖ *Denial* ❖

cial bankruptcy that Congress itself is in a state of gridlock. Major legislation is sitting, without debate, because our representatives know there is no money left to foot the bill. What is Congress doing right now? Basically approving the issuance of new debt to try to fix old problems. It's time for Congress to "just say no" to non-critical expenditures, and start spending its time reviewing and repealing archaic budget-busting laws that are costing taxpayers unbelievable sums of money. The Republicans' "Contract with America" offered great hope in early 1995. But we now see its only business as usual.

The end result of decades of such "family" abuse is staggering. Concentrating on our country as a whole, to see if the situation is functional or dysfunctional, we need only ask one question. What is the current situation with our family, finances, and relationships? Are they working or not?

Our National Family:

- We support the unproductive, constantly cleaning up messes
- 70% of the people are basically broke
- Skyrocketing failures of financial institutions
- Mounting corporate bankruptcies
- Millions of laws attempting to control
- Extremely high tax rates (vs past decades)
- Uncompetitive labor rates compared to other countries

Our National Relationships:

- Try to "fix" other countries
- Critical parent of the world
- "Don't do as we do, do as we say"
- Start armed conflict in Panama while other countries are breaking out in peace
- Nuclear war is still a danger

Our National Finances:

- Inflation (the sign of an abused currency)
- Huge uncollectable foreign loans
- Tremendous trade deficits
- Massive, chronic budget deficits
- The world's largest debtor country

Our economic situation today is even worse than in 1929, when we had *trade surpluses* and *budget surpluses*. And we are in near total denial about it. Those who discuss such problems are put down as "negative thinkers" or called "gloom and doomers." Such responses are similar to what might be expected when a child asks "Daddy, why do you beat Mommy?" Our families are dysfunctional, our companies are dysfunctional, and our country is dysfunctional.

> It is indeed possible for you to deny facts, although it is impossible for you to change them.
> — **A Course In Miracles**

This is not meant to imply that the United States is the only country experiencing such difficulties. The effects are global, even though the magnitude of such problems is most evident here at home. Most other major countries, for example, are experiencing serious financial problems. But we have virtually no control over their difficulties. We can't even deal with our own.

The above might be depressing to many who are only seeing the true situation for the first time. But it's necessary to escape denial and recognize dysfunction before anything can be done about it. Neither does this mean that all of us are headed for the agonies of economic depression. Quite the contrary. *By understanding how debt and our economy truly work, we can see the enormous financial opportunities available.* In fact,

❖ *Denial* ❖

great family fortunes were made during the last deflation. The Kennedy family was a prime example.

After rolling back the veils of denial, we also suddenly realize that *no government can create wealth*. Governments only *influence the transfer* of money from one entity to another. This is not what we've been told, but is true. By knowing how and where money will flow over the next four years we even have a once-in-a-lifetime opportunity to get totally out of debt, prosper financially, and own homes free and clear by 1998. How to correct dysfunctional belief systems about money and achieve financial serenity are the purposes of this book. Regardless of your current situation.

Part Two

THE SOLUTION

1

Our Belief Systems

Humility is a virtue all men preach, none practice, and yet everybody is content to hear.
—John Selden

ONCE WE LOOK beyond the denial, we see that the true financial condition of our country and of most American families is indeed ominous. This requires *humility*. But even the minority who have done well financially must face three critical facts: Everyone will be affected when the debt pyramid starts to crumble; the attractiveness of investments will reverse violently; and those with debt will suffer the most.

Some might sense a twinge of fear at this point. This is not my intent, nor should it be your reaction. In fact, one important objective of this book is to reduce financial fears. By knowing how our economy and investments truly work, you will indeed see the opportunities.

Instead, it would be preferable to ask the question: "How has this situation developed, and more importantly, why have I been kept in the dark so long?"

The answers are twofold. First, *the situation has developed quite slowly*. Had he even breathed the phrase "200 billion dollar deficit," Eisenhower would have been thrown out of the White House in mid-term. Or, as his opponent Adlai

Stevenson once said in jest, "A billion here and a billion there, and sooner or later you're talking about a hell of a lot of money."

A small tax hike here, and one there, "won't even be noticed." A $100 million government expenditure here, and $500 million there won't make that much difference when we consider the total. During the decades our economic mess has slowly been cooking, the smallest child could have easily eaten an entire elephant...a tiny bit at a time.

The second reason "we don't know," is even more important at this time. It's because *we've been listening to the wrong people*! Virtually all of the press, our elected officials, and the financial community is comprised of vested interest groups, who have a specific investment in what you're told. This assumes a source "knows" to begin with.

This doesn't mean everyone is out to get you, or communicates misinformation intentionally. A dysfunctional parent isn't trying to screw up his kids. He is simply manifesting a belief system of which he may or may not even be aware. Or his focus might be too narrow. A stockbroker who's excellent at picking the best stocks might even be proud to recommend a stock that only declines 10%, when other stocks fall 50% in the coming bear market. And it's not unusual for a real estate agent to know very little about how the economy or other investment markets truly function.

We can best achieve the necessary degree of humility about our understanding of investing when we closely look at our sources of information. Where have we learned our belief system that dictates our daily decisions about money and investments? Let's look at each source, one by one.

Sources of Financial Information

THE EDUCATIONAL SYSTEM Did schools teach us about budgeting, debt, inflation and deflation? Our formal education taught us as much about money as it did about parenting...nothing. I've had economists attend my seminars

❖ *Our Belief Systems* ❖

and tell me later they not only agreed with me, but learned things they'd never been taught, even in college.

OUR PARENTS It should be no surprise that we received many of our "tapes" about money and investing from Mom and Dad. And those tapes, including hundreds of do's and don'ts, are still running. Whether our parents were financially successful or not. Whether the grand old ways of making and investing money are still true today or not. Times change.

OUR OWN PERSONAL EXPERIENCES This is a very powerful influence on our current belief system. People can tell us what they want, but what we've actually experienced is our "reality." And the future is expected to be like the past. If you've only been aware of the stock market for 7 years, you probably think that stocks only increase in price. If you're younger that 75, you have never seen real estate fall by 50% as an adult. Unless you're of retirement age, you probably think wages, goods, and services only rise in price.

The foregoing comprise the basic construct of our financial belief system, our ground level "understanding" of how things work. But we are constantly being bombarded by other information sources on a daily basis. Some are even referred to as "experts." Now we must be particularly vigilant. We must determine their underlying purpose before accepting what they say. Do they have a vested interest? What is each's "investment" in what you do with your money?

> No one with a personal investment is a reliable witness, for truth to him has become what he wants it to be.
> **—A Course In Miracles**

ELECTED POLITICIANS The purpose of this group is to stay in office. And if they're in charge now, everything must be great. Right? This also applies to appointed individuals, especially the Chairman of the Federal Reserve Board. Concerning the health of the economy, you already know what these folks will say before they open their mouths. The basic message from this group is "Things are really great and the future is rosy. Re-elect me and I'll keep it that way." This is particularly true at the presidential level. When was the last time you heard a politician admit to a mistake or major problem? Optimism and denial are the norm. Furthermore, it should not be assumed that even presidents fully understand what is happening economically. The greatest example of this was a man who was one of the most heavily-financed presidential candidates in 1980, John Connally. His understanding of deflation and its effects on oil prices were so minimal that he completely missed the deflationary decline in oil prices, and its effect on the Texas economy. He declared bankruptcy in 1988.

The current situation will only change when patchwork solutions to mounting problems no longer work, and a major crisis can no longer be avoided. But I cannot rule out the possibility of true statesmen emerging from the confusion, who accept the fact that all laws involving spending must be closely scrutinized, and most repealed. But this will create pain for those on the receiving side and will be politically and economically unpopular. So the odds are minuscule.

This source of information is all but worthless in gaining a true picture of our economic health, let alone in determining what the future holds. The press also readily regurgitates virtually everything our elected officials say.

POLITICIANS IN WAITING The purpose of these people is to get elected, and their standard line is quite different. Their basic message is: "Things are a mess. Elect me and I'll fix them. And if you help me get elected, I'll remember you when new spending bills are passed and I'm in a position to make appointments." Again, this source is a totally undependable way to obtain a true bearing on economic reality or future developments.

❖ *Our Belief Systems* ❖

STOCKBROKERS The purpose of stockbrokers is to earn commissions on sales of securities. No one can object to one's right to earn a living. But when deciding how to invest, stockbrokers are generally a poor source of information. This is because some investments yield far greater commissions than others. Would a car salesman prefer to sell you a Cadillac or Chevy compact? By the same token, the most appropriate investment might carry an extremely small commission. I believe this to be one of the primary reasons why brokers rarely recommend treasury bonds to small clients. For example, one could buy a half-million dollars of treasury bonds for only $500 in commissions. As a seller of securities in the same situation, might you instead suggest something that generated ten times such commission amounts? Perhaps stocks? Furthermore, if the client wants to use mutual funds for buying stocks, brokers simply don't offer no-load funds.

The manner in which stockbrokers make overall investment recommendations is also quite interesting. The major brokerage houses centralize their research and recommendations, generally in New York City. This information is then disseminated to the local branches, who then contact individual clients. The first question is would you expect them to call you first? Or would they first contact their major institutional clients, starting in New York? By the time the small investor receives the information, prices have often already appreciated. It is also rare for major brokerage houses to recommend total sale of certain types of investments. Their influence is so great that a panic would surely ensue, even if they were prescient enough to see a major problem developing, like the Crash of 1987. One major question for any stockbroker is, "Were your clients spared that massive decline?"

INSURANCE AGENTS Most people cannot afford to self-insure, and need insurance. But an interesting trend has developed over the past several years. Most insurance agents also now sell securities. Their major securities products are heavily commissioned mutual funds, annuities, and strange combinations of insurance/investments. Having the license to sell securities does not mean an individual knows how the economy changes and which security is most appropriate for the future. And again, those products carrying the highest commission will naturally be favored. I also oppose the sales of insurance products for "savings" or investment purposes. If you need insurance, buy insurance. If you want to invest, invest. Never mix the two. The objective of an insurance agent, regarding investment, is again commissions.

FINANCIAL PLANNERS It is critical to classify financial planners into two categories. The first is a fee-only planner. These people charge you by the hour or per review, and don't make their money on the sale of investments recommended. Such professionals can be quite valuable in helping you make sense out of your finances, and in helping you develop goals and how to achieve them. Make sure, however, that your planner understands how the economy changes and why, which is often not the case.

The second type of planner will charge you very little, if anything, for a review. The purpose, of course, is to earn commissions on the sale of securities that are conveniently recommended as exactly appropriate to your needs. Their list of products is usually quite similar to those of insurance agents active in security sales.

CERTIFIED PUBLIC ACCOUNTANTS One primary purpose of such professionals is to assist you in preparing tax returns and minimizing your taxes. I have more respect for CPAs as professionals than those in perhaps any other industry, primarily because they do an excellent job of self-regulation.

There is, however, a growing trend in this industry to also sell commissioned investments. Few CPAs are currently doing this, but I suggest you treat such individuals with the same caution as you would most insurance agents. One as-

❖ *Our Belief Systems* ❖

sumption investors make with CPAs is that just because they deal with money they know investing. In fact, when a CPA recommends a certain investment, state laws usually require he be licensed as a financial planner. If your accountant makes specific investment recommendations, you might want to ask this question.

Despite the great respect I have for this profession, the greatest financial disasters I've ever seen were created by CPAs. These cases involved such aggressive attempts to minimize their client's current year taxes, that tax-advantaged investments were recommended which made no economic sense. Over the next few years, partnerships and real estate bought strictly for tax purposes will likely be the worst investments you'll ever make.

BANKERS As with CPAs, just because an individual deals with money doesn't mean he understands economic change and thus timely or appropriate investment. And the primary purpose of a banker is to sell investments offered by the bank, thus attracting deposits, and then investing or loaning out such monies at a profit. So he concentrates on investments offered by his bank. A Ford dealer will not likely recommend a Chevrolet to a customer. For this reason, you should not consider most bankers as unbiased sources of investment advice.

INVESTMENT ADVISERS Advisers often come from the brokerage industry, or sometimes are self-taught, using other established investment advisers to develop their investment acumen. Their organizations provide investment research, often to the above people, and to businesses and individuals, for a price. This research is sold in written research reports, by direct consultation, by newsletters, by money management services, and sometimes with telephone "hotline" services. In its purest form, this source of information can be among the least-prejudiced available.

It is, however, necessary to also divide this group into two categories. Those who refuse to sell securities can be very helpful. But others develop fascinating scenarios only to justify the sale of commissioned securities, gold coins, etc. Careful review of their operating procedures or (if available) their newsletter will quickly tell you if a vested interest is present. Most typical is an attractive newsletter telling you what will happen economically, followed at the end with how to purchase those gold coins, diamonds, etc. from their company, to satisfy such requirements.

NEWSPAPERS I find it interesting that anything in print is often immediately considered fact. Avoid this trap. The biggest problem with most daily newspapers is they tell what has already happened. What happened yesterday is of no value whatsoever in choosing your investments. You must *predict the future* to be an astute and successful investor. Never forget this. You should therefore use newspapers to help you identify NEW trends. Those concentrating on business will be the most helpful in doing this. The primary purpose of newspapers is to sell newspapers and advertising, not to make you money.

When IRAs first came out, I was asked by a newspaper to write an article summarizing how they worked and the best places to open such an account. For reasons now clearly obvious, I stated S&Ls weren't good choices. The paper's largest advertiser, an S&L, canceled their advertising! The account was later reinstated, but *this is how the real world of vested interests works*, even in the media.

BOOKS Always, repeat, always determine in advance who wrote the book, and whether the author has any biased opinion or vested interest in what he relates. Use the same rules discussed above. One problem with books is it often takes a great deal of time to write the work, and more time to get it published and distributed. So regarding timeliness of certain investments, remember it could be severely dated. Books can also be a good contrary indicator. During the early 1980s, for example, store shelves were overflowing with books telling you how to profit from inflation. That alone should have told you that inflation had run its course. *Any investment trend that is fully identified will virtually always reverse itself.* More on this later. So use books to learn more about how certain investments work and to develop strategies to improve your results, always keeping in mind that you are trying to predict the future. Of course some authors simply don't know what they're talking about. So use this source with caution. The primary purpose of most books is to sell books.

MAGAZINES A few decades ago, one or two magazines held the lion's share of the entire market. Today you can buy magazines detailing any type of specialty area imaginable. But unlike fishing and computers, beware of investment magazines. Again, you can use them to develop strategies and techniques for better investing, assuming they understand the big picture, which is often not the case. But never, repeat, never use them to determine timeliness of investments. By the time a magazine completes its research, decides that a certain stock or investment is truly appropriate, and finally gets it into print, the professionals will have fully priced that item. The primary purpose of magazines is to sell magazines and advertising, not to make you money.

BUSINESS TELEVISION Particularly with the advent of cable television, you can literally overdose with investment information. *CNBC* is currently very prominent. Much of their coverage is excellent, some can lead to paralysis by analysis. They interview numerous guests every day. Should you use such information? Apply the same guidelines you would based on our prior discussion. If a brokerage house representative is being interviewed, you won't expect him to say "Sell all stocks, they're heading down!" Or if they interview the

Chairman of the Federal Reserve Board, don't expect him to say "The party's over. The economy is going to hell in a handbasket." Be vigilant, and always look for vested interests.

Wall Street Week has been around for years. Again, use the same vigilance you would if the individual weren't on national television. But the biggest problem with television investment programs (and magazines) is too many people own televisions or buy those magazines. For profitable investment, *you must see something that no one or few other people see.* Follow the crowd and the professionals will wipe you out. For example, the following article appeared in *Fact Magazine* in the early 1980s:

> "Last year, an Institute for Econometric Research study showed that stocks recommended on TV's Wall Street Week rose sharply in the two weeks before a show but fell afterward. Now a new Bernard Baruch College study of 202 Wall Street Week recommendations made over a two year period shows that touted stocks fell an average 7.5% over the two months following the show. The only time the stocks rose was on the day following the show."

What Everyone Knows Isn't Worth Knowing

Whether it be a stock everyone likes, accepted opinion by the investment community, or what all the television shows or investment magazines decide is best, never follow the crowd. In other words, "What everyone knows or believes about an investment, isn't worth knowing." In fact, a *growing minority viewpoint* is the basis for greatest investment profits. This sounds crazy, but it's true.

Let's consider an example. Assume we could construct a perfect survey, and choose 100 people who were perfectly representative of all people. Our question is simply, "Are stocks a good investment right now?" (Choose your invest-

❖ *Our Belief Systems* ❖

ment: Real estate, gold, anything will work.) Let's assume all 100 people said yes. Based only on that response, would you tend to buy or sell stocks? Think about this for a minute.

You would sell, and sell fast. Why? Our survey was perfect, so everyone thinks stocks are good investments. A vast majority don't have any money or stocks, so they can be ignored. But our perfect survey told us all active investors also believe they're great investments. If this is their belief, wouldn't they have already bought? At this point, are there more potential sellers or potential buyers? Everyone is a potential seller and no one is a potential buyer. There is only one way the market can go, and that's down.

Contrast this with gold investments in the late 1970s. Only a tiny percentage of the population would have even considered buying gold. It took little additional interest to send the price skyrocketing. Almost everyone was a potential buyer.

What does majority opinion say today about real estate, stocks, bonds, and the economy? Of course you would never base your investments on this information alone, but be extremely cautious when following the crowd. Simply remember, what everyone knows in investing isn't worth knowing.

Worse, what is heard, seen, or read is often passed on to others. Who was the source? "They." Now it becomes unquestioned fact. *Always* identify the source and any vested interests, and beware of majority opinion.

Add a constant barrage of messages from the above sources to a questionable basic belief system, and the result is a bizarre concept of money, investing, and the economy.

Much can make no sense at all. But it comprises our belief system, made up of hundreds of "facts." How many of the following messages are part of your belief system?

> "A penny saved is a penny earned."
> "You haven't got the brains God gave a goose."
> "Renting is like stuffing money down a rat hole."
> "Real estate always goes up in value."

"They're not making any more land."
"I have to buy a house to get a write-off on taxes."
"The stock market is only a big gamble."
"Stocks are down, but they'll go back up; they always have."
"Borrow and pay it back in cheaper dollars."
"Never invest more than you can afford to lose."
"I'm not an investor, I only put money into CDs."
"Money is the root of all evil."
"He's a gold bug."
"The deficit is only what we owe ourselves."
"'They' will force interest rates lower..."
"Never a lender nor a borrower be."
"Don't trust anyone."

Now, go back and ask yourself, what was the probable source of each message, and could that source have had a vested interest in such a belief? Or, did that person truly understand? None of the above are appropriate during all periods, and most are downright insane statements.

Is it any wonder you've bought investments you didn't understand, have lost money, or are up to your eyeballs in debt? Or perhaps your parental messages were so strong and negative, and your self-esteem so low, that you've been flirting with poverty for years. Even if "successful," but owe a lot of money, you're in for a rude awakening over the next four years.

The bottom line is reaching the frame of mind that "I don't know." Again, one major test is "Are my finances working or not?" And are you 100% certain tomorrow's best investments will be the same as yesterday's? Why?

All it takes, if for only an instant, is one decision... "There must be another way." At that point you've reached enough humility to open your mind just far enough to consider an alternative—a new way of looking at things that makes complete sense.

❖ *Our Belief Systems* ❖

One word of caution. Don't try to fit your current money belief system into that presented over the next eleven chapters. It won't fit. Instead, I invite you to compare your current belief system with what is presented only after completing all chapters. At that point you can choose which makes the most sense, and place probabilities on which is the most true. Then commit those percentages to the strategy presented and to your current approach. But be careful of your current belief system. It is based on dubious sources with questionable vested interests. In the end, regardless of what has occurred in the past, future results are the final measure of truth.

Incidentally, any time you place money with another person or financial institution, you are investing. This includes bank deposits, a loan to a relative, the purchase of real estate, annuities, and virtually any other money transfer.

2

The Facts Revealed

One door never shuts but another opens.
—Anon

ONCE WE HAVE developed some financial humility, it is possible to open our minds to new approaches. To obtain that humility it was necessary to realize that most of our earlier and current sources of information about money, the economy, and investing came from unreliable sources. That our belief system in these areas might not be true.

As we learned the real facts, we might have even felt cheated or angry. But that was the past. It serves no purpose to blame others or ourselves, but to simply choose again and start anew. This establishes *hope*. It is necessary, however, to make sure our new sources of information have no vested interest (investment) in how we accumulate and handle our money. Certain investment advisers seem to be the best choice. This was my approach starting many years ago, and it served me well. I carefully avoided those who were simply trying to justify sales of investments, and went out of my way to find the best minds in the world to learn the truth about money and investing. I will now share this with you.

Regardless of whether you have no money left over at month's end, or have accumulated a great deal of wealth, your opportunities are enormous over the next four years. This is because we are already starting to experience a period of extremely rapid and unprecedented economic change. If you enter this period knowing how money and the economy work, you have the opportunity to reach financial serenity by 1998. But the old ways of investing and managing money simply won't work.

Even if you "can't make ends meet," would you be interested in knowing there are ways to turn every $1 you can put your hands on today into $20-30 in four years, after inflation? Do you think you just might be able to carve a few dollars out of your budget, or make a little extra money on the side to do this?

Such incredible gains might sound preposterous right now. You will soon decide otherwise. But it requires a new way of thinking. In fact, similar gains were made over the past several years. Let me explain. Our approach doesn't involve real estate, but assume you bought a house for $50,000 in 1970 with 10% down. Today it's worth $150,000, and you only had $5,000 of your own money in the property. If you sold, and paid off the mortgage, you grew $1 into $30. Taxes must, of course, also be paid. But this was possible because you made an appropriate investment, perhaps accidentally, during a period when it made sense to borrow heavily, leveraging your position. And inflation helped you do this.

Understanding debt and inflation is the key. But inflation has also created one of the greatest illusions of our time. Consider, for example, someone who bought and sold the exact same property as above, but paid cash (no debt). The house increased in value from $50,000 to $150,000. Right? Wrong. The house did not appreciate in value at all! Because during that period the value, the purchasing power, of the dollar fell by two-thirds. Considering inflation, that $150,000 would today buy the exact same as $50,000 in 1970. But in this second example, the investment was actually a loser, because taxes on "illusionary gains" were paid. Inflation is perhaps the greatest hoax that could ever be pulled on a consuming public. It

❖ *The Facts Revealed* ❖

helped the heavy debtor produce incredible real estate gains, but punished the cash-based buyer.

So our first basic step in learning about money and investing is to know exactly how inflation works, when to use debt, and how to prepare for the new period of something called deflation. Your basic training starts right now.

Inflation and Deflation Explained

It's first necessary to forget current definitions of inflation. I've even known a businessman who was one step away from becoming Vice-President of a huge multinational company, as well as economics majors, who didn't understand how inflation really works. In particular, totally forget the term disinflation. The term means nothing.

Let's start with a few simple definitions. They might be slightly different from what is found in some textbooks, but our objective is clarity for the average person, not a doctorate degree.

MONETARY INFLATION is a significant *increase* in the supply of money.

This might sound innocuous enough, but let's consider the ramifications. Assume all the wheat in the world this year sold for an average of $6 a bushel. If all the farmers in the world decided to plant nothing but wheat next year, and produced three times that amount, what would you expect to happen to prices? If demand stayed about the same, and there were three times as much wheat, wouldn't you expect wheat to fall in value to about $2? This is exactly what happened to the dollar over the last twenty years. There was a huge increase in the supply of money, and the dollar's value dropped by two-thirds, as measured by the Consumer Price Index.

PRICE INFLATION is an apparent general *increase* in prices, when caused by monetary inflation.

We measure prices in terms of dollars. And if the value of a dollar drops, prices *appear* to rise. If we treated wheat as a "currency" or barter tool, and priced everything in bushels of wheat this year, and in bushels of wheat next year (from our example), prices would seem to triple. This is exactly what happened over the last two decades, as prices measured in dollars appeared to triple. We're accustomed to using pints, feet, inches and other units of measure which don't change. But using something that constantly changes as a unit of measure is very deceiving. This reality and these two simple definitions will go far in correcting a faulty belief, and more importantly, prepare you to understand what has been occurring over the last several decades. Please think about this for a minute, to make sure you understand this important concept.

MONETARY DEFLATION is a significant *decrease* in the supply of money.

This always occurs after long periods of inflation, as debts go bad, and describes the future. The results are exactly the opposite from inflation. When something becomes more rare, the value increases. During deflationary periods the purchasing power of the dollar increases.

PRICE DEFLATION is an apparent general *decrease* in prices, when caused by monetary deflation.

Measuring prices in terms of something that is *increasing in value* makes it appear that prices are *falling*. But again, we're only seeing the effects of a changing unit of measurement. Remember that this not only affects what we buy. It influences anything denominated in dollars. Including investments and wages and salaries.

The only thing not directly affected is debt and its repayment. After incurring a monthly payment of only $300 on a

❖ *The Facts Revealed* ❖

house mortgage in 1970, repayment became dramatically easier as wages and salaries "increased" because of inflation over the years. Can you imagine how a monthly mortgage payment of $1000 would feel if deflation cut your wages by two-thirds over the next four years? And that would only take us back to 1970 dollar levels. Our current inflationary binge has been in place much longer than that. Any deflation completely removes all the debt created during the prior inflationary period. This deflation will return dollar value and "prices" to where they began in the 1960s. Deflation is a natural response to inflation, and the inflation/deflation cycle has been repeating itself for centuries.

Let me share one example about deflation. And never forget it. When inflation turns into deflation, massive changes occur in the price of certain investments. Most drop sharply in "price," but a few others rise dramatically. We will later describe which securities are involved, but assume you invested $1 today in those specific investments which rise in value. As the economy snaps and deflation (a negative Consumer Price Index) takes hold, your investment increases sharply in price. Your unique investment increases 60% a year for five years. This might sound preposterous. (Hint: The stock market crash on October 19, 1987, was an excellent one-day example of deflation. This particular investment increased in price from $40 to $6000 in that one single day.) At a more conservative 60% growth a year, in five years your $1 grows to $10 (or $6.50 in four years).

But if deflation only increases the value of the dollar back to 1970 levels, each *safe* dollar will buy three times as much. So your money has $20 - $30 in purchasing power. Deflation presents wonderful investment opportunities, if you understand the process and specifically choose the correct investments.

But you still don't know what causes the inflation/deflation process. We said that increases and decreases in the supply of money are the true cause of both price inflation and price deflation. Let's see exactly how that works.

The supply of money today rises and falls because of the Reserve Banking System and borrowing. There is one critical definition related to this discussion of banks:

THE MINIMUM RESERVE REQUIREMENT is the percentage of any deposit a bank must place in reserves (about 10%).

We now have all the definitions we need to describe how banks operate, and how the supply of money rises and falls. It's time to play bank, so you can personally experience how this process works.

Assume you and your family members own several banks. I come into your bank and deposit $100. Based on a 10% Minimum Reserve Requirement, you must place about $10 in reserves. What do you do with the rest? You can either invest the remaining $90 or lend it to someone, to make money on your deposit and pay bills and shareholders. You decide to make it available for new loans. Mr. Creditworthy needs $90 to buy that new sports coat. You make the loan, perhaps via a credit card, and he buys the coat at Clothes R Us. At the end of the day, that business deposits the $90 in Dad's Bank. We now have $190 in total deposits. (My $100 plus $90 by the store.)

Wow!...A new deposit. So dad sets aside $9 on reserve (10% of the new deposit) and lends $81 to Mrs. Creditworthy. She uses the loan to buy jewelry at her local department store. The store deposits the $81 in Mom's Bank. We now have $271 in total deposits in our banking system.

Another new deposit. Mom puts 10% (about $8) on reserve, and lends $73 to Susie Spendthrift, who goes down and buys some new compact discs at Sound Heaven. At the end of the day, the record store deposits the $73 in your bank. We now have $344 in total bank deposits.

I think you can see what's happening. That original $100 is working its way through the system, and deposits and the supply of money are growing like bunny rabbits. When we

❖ *The Facts Revealed* ❖

take this to completion we end up with $1000 in total deposits and $100 (10%) in reserves. The money supply has grown from $100 to $1000.

Deposits	$100	90	81.00	72.90	.....$1000
Less 10% Reserve	-10	-9	-8.10	-7.29	100
New Loans	90	81	72.90	65.61	900

This is how the money supply grows today—with borrowing via the banks. This is the true cause of inflation. The reverse occurs during a deflation. When a loan goes bad, banks must write off such amounts against their net worth and capital. This has the effect of reducing the amount of money for future lending. Less cash is available. During a period of loan defaults and a poor economy, prudence also dictates decreased lending. If not, such institutions can encounter regulatory problems. To raise cash a bank might even be forced to sell investments, such as stocks, bonds, or repossessed real estate. This has the effect of further reducing prices within these markets, and decreasing borrowers' collateral for subsequent loans. In sum, the money supply is equally leveraged in its ability to contract as well as to expand.

One can determine how liquid, or brittle, the banking system is at any point, by determining what percentage banks are "loaned out." When financial institutions have lent more than 80% of all deposits, like today, the system is extremely vulnerable to bad loans, and horrors, the possibility of a run on the bank. When the system is very liquid, and only 20-30% of deposits are loaned out like in the early 1940s following the last depression, such institutions are much more capable of dealing with surprises.

This process also goes far in explaining why banks, savings and loans, and credit unions are experiencing such massive problems. Our typical "sources of information" tend to concentrate on bad management, fraud, and other types of explanations. You can now see the true underlying cause is a shaky financial structure, due to very low banking liquidity.

The above example did not cover "deposit insurance." Financial institutions also place a tiny percentage of deposits into an insurance corporation. Depositors are often content in knowing that deposits are insured. The Federal Savings & Loan Insurance Corporation (FSLIC) is already bankrupt, and another insuring body has taken its place. The FDIC can only cover about 1% of total bank deposits with insurance. In fact, such insurance corporations were only designed to cover the one-off type of failures which periodically occur. They were never destined to bail out the entire banking system. And from the above, you can see the entire financial system is tightly entwined, especially when vulnerable due to low liquidity.

But, you say, the system is protected by the full faith and credit of the United States Government. As if they're in any better financial condition than the banking system itself. I certainly wouldn't pick the largest debtor country in the world, with its massive budget and trade deficits, to stand behind me. Remember one thing. Banks are businesses. They take in a product at wholesale (money deposits at low interest rates) and sell it at retail (loans at higher interest rates). Once the public demands that the government quit trying to bail out every major company in the country, to keep itself from going under, or our leaders in Washington reach their senses, it will finally be realized Uncle Sam couldn't possibly guarantee deposits to $100,000. And why should the average taxpayer (the majority) be expected to back the largest of depositors (the minority)? Fully expect this guarantee to be lowered to the $10,000 to $20,000 range, or eventually lower, as denial falls away, debts start going bad with increasing speed, and reality starts to prevail.

❖ *The Facts Revealed* ❖

The Fed Factor

The banking system plays a critical role in the entire process. But we haven't yet discussed another factor which has been extremely active in causing inflation, at least until 1986. The Federal Reserve Board has used the banking system to try to control the economy. Picture a recessionary period. Businesses and individuals are complaining about bad business and high interest rates. It's time to crank up the banking system even further. Simply remember one thing. The Federal Reserve Bank also loans money to banks.

DISCOUNT RATE is the interest rate the Fed charges banks when they borrow money from the government.

If the Federal Reserve wants to move the economy out of recession, one thing they do is lower the Discount Rate. After all, if the banks can borrow money at a lower rate, they can charge lower interest rates to borrowers. Right? And if interest rates are lower, won't people borrow more, and therefore buy more, strengthening the economy? This is the objective. Even if it leads to another, higher, wave of inflation.

Another critical action is the purchase, by the Federal Reserve Bank, of treasury bonds and treasury bills. When the Fed buys these securities from banks, this adds money to the banking system, just like our original $100 deposit. But this time we're talking about millions or billions of dollars, that might be only computer numbers, or "money" which never existed prior. As they pay dollars for the securities, this money enters the banking system. And the bunny rabbits start growing again, this time by the millions.

One other tool is for the Fed to actually lower the Minimum Reserve Requirement. Money supply can grow much more quickly if banks have to set aside less on reserve. This action is rarely taken, but when it does occur it causes massive changes in the value of investments.

Of course the Fed can also take the opposite steps to slow down the economy or decrease inflation. 1980 was a perfect example of this. Inflation was clearly getting out of hand, voters were screaming, and it was time to do something.

The first Fed action was to dramatically increase the Discount Rate. Banks were forced to greatly increase interest rates to borrowers. With high interest rates, people borrowed less, therefore spent less, and the economy braked severely. As money supply dropped, inflation eventually came down hard.

The Fed also started *selling* government securities. Money generated from those sales was taken out of the banking system, which made less money available for loans. This also had the effect of decreasing money supply.

Increasing the Minimum Reserve Requirement was not a step taken during that period. But the overall effect was a sharp severe recession that broke the back of inflation.

The Powerless Federal Reserve Board

With such enormous power to influence interest rates, the money supply, and the economy, the Fed can prevent downturns in the economy. Right? Until 1986, yes. Today, no. Here's the problem: In 1986 we became the world's largest debtor country. This important event changed the identity of our major creditors (government bondholders). We are no longer a closed system, depending only on domestic buyers of government bonds to finance our government's voracious needs for money. We now have to keep German and particularly Japanese investors happy, so they keep buying our government bonds. How do you keep them happy? By offering interest rates high enough so they continue lending us money (buying our bonds).

When the economy starts slowing, the Fed naturally decreases interest rates to increase borrowing from banks, move spending higher, and keep the money supply and the economy growing. But what effect would this have on Japanese and

❖ *The Facts Revealed* ❖

German bond buyers? They would find our rates less attractive, and buy fewer bonds. If Washington is not careful, they can lower rates to spur the economy, but jeopardize their ability to borrow enough money to keep the federal government operating.

In fact, our economic future is now more dependent on what happens in Japan than on what our Fed decides. This was illustrated in 1987 with the first leg of the coming stock market crash. To see what triggered that sharp crash, it's necessary you assume the role of a Japanese investor.

You had lent huge sums of money to the world's largest debtor country, by buying U.S. bonds. But you saw the value of your investment falling, because the dollar dropped against the Yen. To bring your money back to Japan, you need to sell bonds, and then buy Yen with those dollars. Fewer could be bought because the Yen was rising against the dollar. You lost more than 10% on your investment for this reason alone. So you sold bond holdings or quit buying new bonds.

Market interest rates started rising because of less bond demand. (During normal periods, you Japanese often buy some 30% of every new treasury bond offering.) To make bond interest rates more attractive, the Fed raised the Discount Rate. Higher interest rates are poison to heavily-indebted corporations, and future demand for their products and services became questionable. Everyone sold stocks, driving their price down 35% (22% in only one day). Everyone had simply opened his eyes and seen that the American emperor had no clothes. The very next day, on October 20, 1987, it was later revealed that our financial system almost failed. That is how tenuous our financial system is right now. With the Japanese stock market in serious trouble, the Nikkei alone could trigger the next worldwide deflation.

Our spendthrift government has backed us into a corner. We no longer have control over our own monetary policy. But let's assume interest rates are lowered, without causing overseas lenders to boycott the purchase of our government's debt vehicles. Would there be an automatic increase in borrowing, the money supply, and inflation? No, not if one or a combination of the following occur:

- If banks won't make sufficient loans to those wanting to borrow
- If people won't borrow because of a growing fear of debt or worries about job security
- If old loans are going bad faster than new loans are being created

The first item has attracted much press, and until 1994 banks were notoriously stingy in granting many types of loans. Now that short-term interest rates have increased sharply, fewer potential borrowers qualify for many loans. Credit card debt is currently growing by leaps and bounds, and many people are even using plastic to buy consumables such as groceries. The hangover from this credit addiction will begin to occur by early 1996, as millions of credit card junkies find it impossible to repay such debt and declare bankruptcy. Many banks are no longer making business and commercial real estate loans. Let's see how debt (or its absence) influences the "price" of this single item.

You want to sell a commercial property for $300,000. You find a buyer willing to put up $50,000 in cash, but needing to finance the rest. Banks won't make the loan. What is the real value of your property? Upon final analysis, it's only worth what someone will pay in cash. Before this deflation is over, this will occur with virtually everything. As prices fall, no bank will want to lend money to buy something that will soon fall below the value of the loan. Many companies have also gone back to the well and been refused additional credit. This alone is increasing the company bankruptcy rate. At the same time, more people are becoming ineligible for loans of any type.

The second item above is also occurring. Even if their credit rating is just fine, every day more people are "just saying no" to new debt. They are jumping off the debt treadmill that

❖ *The Facts Revealed* ❖

is strangling them. They're going cold turkey, finally recognizing their debt addiction. Some fear loss of jobs. Others are selling indebted assets, even at sharp discounts, before prices plunge even further.

Adjusting for Inflation

Because the purchasing power of the dollar changes so dramatically, it's necessary to adjust for fluctuations in any dollar transaction or investment. This includes the prices of goods or services in general. Only when we use constant dollars can we adjust for a changing unit of measure.

The first thing we need is a record of dollar value over time. The Consumer Price Index is the most popular index of dollar purchasing value:

CONSUMER PRICE INDEX BY YEAR (December)
(Source: U.S. Department of Labor)

YEAR	CPI	YEAR	CPI	YEAR	CPI
1962	30.3	1973	44.4	1984	102.7
1963	30.6	1974	49.3	1985	106.4
1964	31.0	1975	53.8	1986	108.0
1965	31.6	1976	56.9	1987	115.4
1966	32.5	1977	60.6	1988	120.5
1967	33.4	1978	65.2	1989	126.1
1968	34.8	1979	72.7	1990	133.8
1969	36.7	1980	82.5	1991	137.9
1970	38.8	1981	90.9	1992	141.9
1971	40.5	1982	96.4	1993	145.8
1972	41.8	1983	99.3	1994	150.4

The first thing we notice is today's dollar only buys 21% of what it did in 1964 (31.0/150.4). In other words, 79% of the dollar's purchasing power has been destroyed over the last 30 years.

We also need a simple formula to determine true price

changes of anything, including investments. The following allows true calculation of the percentage increase, or decrease, of anything's value. True Percentage Return on Investment (% ROI) is:

$$\% \text{ ROI} = \frac{(E - T)\, I1/I2}{S} - 1 \times 100$$

Rearranging, we get:

$$\% \text{ ROI} = \frac{(I1)(E - T)}{(I2)(S)(.01)} - 100$$

Where:
- I1 = Inflation Index (CPI) at the time of original investment
- I2 = Inflation Index (CPI) today, or when investment was sold
- S = Starting investment (or original "price" of something)
- E = Ending investment (or today's "price" of something)
- T = Taxes paid

Example #1

We bought a $10,000 one-year certificate of deposit in December, 1988, and it matured in December, 1989. So from the chart we see that I1 = 120.5, and I2 = 126.1. Assume it paid 7.5% interest. So our starting investment was $10,000 = S and our ending investment was this amount plus 7.5% interest

($750), for an ending investment of $10,750 = E. Assume a combined total state and federal tax rate of 25% on the $750 and we get $187.50 = T.

By plugging these numbers into the equation we get .93%. So after adjusting for taxes and the depreciating value of a dollar, we received less than 1% real return. Do such investments truly compensate for the risk of investing money in financial institutions that will soon again be failing at record rates?

Example #2:

We bought a stock in 1966 for $90, and sold it at $280 at the absolute highest price it reached in 1987 before the crash. (If we multiply by 10 we get the respective levels of the Dow Jones Industrial Average.) Again assume a 25% total state and federal tax rate, and a 2% commission to buy and again to sell. Our original investment was $10,000 = S.

We received a 4.3% average (very typical) dividend every year, paid 25% taxes on dividends and placed the remainder into a money market fund that averaged 7% interest a year. Every year we paid taxes on that interest at 25%. After taxes, we had $16,507 in that account when we sold our stock. (This calculation is not shown.) We received $29,879 net from the stock sale. A 25% tax on the gain was $5,020 = T. We've already subtracted tax on dividends and money fund interest so the ending investment is $29,879 plus $16,507 = $46,386 = E. I1 was 32.5 in 1966, and I2 was 115.4 in 1987 from the chart.

If we hadn't paid taxes directly out of the money fund, we would appear to have a total of $30,010 in that fund plus $29,879 from the stock sale for a total of $59,889. That looks like a great deal for a $10,000 investment. But by plugging all the above numbers into the equation, we end up, after taxes and inflation, with a real percentage gain of 16.5%. That's less than 1% a year (.73%) real return. And that assumes we didn't suffer a massive decline in the 1987 crash. A $90 growth stock that didn't pay dividends would had to have increased in price to $413 just to break even. (This also means that without any dividends, the Dow Industrials would have to have increased to 4130 in 1987, just to break even.) So much for long-term stock investing.

Of course this formula can also be used to measure the real percentage price change of anything from bread to new cars. But it does not compensate for a drop in quality that has generally occurred with numerous products over the last few decades.

This is how illusions work. And inflation is perhaps the greatest illusion possible in investing and how we price things. These examples should hammer home the fact that prices seldom rise, but inflation is instead a loss in the value of a dollar.

Myths About Inflation

Many entities have been blamed for inflation: Big business, labor unions, higher oil prices, etc. Inflation is caused by the government itself, with the help of the banking system. Do you remember the WIN buttons under the Ford administration? WIN meant Whip Inflation Now. We were all asked to do our part to tame the inflation monster. Exactly how were we supposed to assist in this novel task? This was perhaps the most asinine suggestion ever proposed by the White House, even if it sounded good at the time and appeared patriotic. I'll leave you to ponder the motivation behind this action. Have you ever heard of a mushroom meeting? You put everyone in the dark, down in the basement, and feed them tons of bull____.

But wait a minute. Does this mean those "evil oil producers" weren't responsible for inflation when they jacked up oil prices in the 1970s? That's right. As they saw the value of the dollar plummet via inflation, they decided to catch up by increasing prices, and felt they were in a position to go even further. But this didn't affect U.S. inflation. This might not be obvious, so let's take a closer look.

❖ *The Facts Revealed* ❖

Most households spend everything they earn. If your monthly income is $2000 and you spend $2000 every month, perhaps $100 a month goes for oil-based products, particularly gasoline. If oil prices tripled, you'd be forced to spend $300 a month for such items. But suddenly you have $200 less to buy other things. So demand for other things must drop, and so will their price. You push down on the waterbed here; it rises over there. If you don't spend everything you earn, you can buy fewer investments, real estate, etc. It makes no difference. But there's only one way for *prices in general* to increase. That's when someone is messing with your money system.

It's even possible for inflation to occur when gold is used as money. In the 16th century Spain was hauling gold by the shipload from the New World to that country. Prices took off, because the money supply increased.

Money can be inflated even when the total amount of gold or silver is constant. The government simply calls in all the precious metal coins, melts them down, and reissues a greater number of coins that contain greater amounts of other, cheaper metals. Has the U.S. government ever pulled such a trick? (Hint—silver coins after 1963.) Incidentally, what is the greatest inflation rate ever recorded in the United States? Inflation in 1974 and 1980 was a far cry from the record. As inflation surpassed 200%, we completely destroyed the Continental Dollar two centuries ago. And few people remember the Greenback from a hundred years ago.

I am also incensed by the government's implication they can "bring inflation back down to 0%." This first assumes they still have some degree of control, without destroying the economy, which the above sharply contradicts. And since inflation is a function of money supply growth or contraction, why should the growth of money have a floor at 0%? It either grows or contracts. There's nothing magical about 0%. Decades of inflation simply culminates in deflation (a negative inflation rate), as the debt pyramid crumbles. We then start all over again.

Summary

So there you have it. You now understand inflation and deflation. You also understand how debt is the key to both. It's also now obvious how tenuous our current financial situation is, and how little it can be manipulated as in the past.

If you don't understand the process, you are totally at the mercy of the system. If you understand and don't say anything, you can't complain. It's simply time to become actors instead of reactors. It's time to stop abdicating our lives to a government that will "fix things." Governments do not and cannot "fix" anything, at least in terms of economics and money. When you take a close look at government itself and how it operates, you will again come to one simple but true fact: *Governments cannot create wealth.* They can only *influence its transfer* from one group or individual to another.

Do you want to be on the receiving side, or remain in the dark, in a mushroom meeting? By understanding money, how it works, and how it doesn't work, you've taken the first step towards financial sanity and serenity. Regardless of your current situation.

This chapter was quite technical in nature, but true. Make sure you understand the major points before proceeding. Understanding how inflation and deflation work forms the basis for the much easier steps that follow. Go back and review this chapter, as many times as necessary, until you fully understand it. Discuss it with others who possess the same book or similar references until you're comfortable with the basics. Then continue without delay.

3

The Harmony of Business Cycles

*Always fall in with what you're asked to accept.
Take what is given, and make it over your way.
My aim in life has always been to hold my own
with whatever's going. Not against: with.*
—Robert Frost

IT'S NOW TIME to accept the fact that forces well beyond our control exercise great power over our personal economies and finances. But even if we cannot control those forces, if we understand them we can turn problems into opportunities.

Yet our actions often do not coincide with the ebb and flow of things. We buy stocks and insist they rise, even as the economy starts to exhale. We buy bonds and watch in amazement as their prices fall, as inflation again starts to awaken. We assume great quantities of debt, via real estate or credit cards, just as the dollar finally starts its generational and cyclical increase in value. We quit our job and start our own business right before the next recession. Even huge corporations often base the next 20 years on what has been in place the prior two decades.

Certain rhythms we naturally accept. We don't expect dusk at noon; we don't expect it to snow in the summertime or leaves to fall in the spring. Why do we sometimes try to swim upstream with our businesses and our investments? It's because we're simply not aware of, or have never even been exposed to, the natural cycles affecting these areas.

But where does this fit in our new approach to money and investing? Cycles help us do the one and only thing necessary to make timely investments—*predict the future*.

Make sure you totally understand that the recent past means precious little when it comes to investment. A fund that made 20% a year over the last four years could well be the biggest loser imaginable over the next four. Particularly if we are on the verge of quantum change in a new direction, which we are. Your investments today will rise or fall based only on what happens in the immediate future.

The Deflation Cycle

By understanding past investment cycles we can better know where we are today, and project with better accuracy what will unfold tomorrow. The most powerful cycle I have researched was discovered by a gentleman in the 1920s. This phenomenon also bears his name. It is called the Kondratieff Wave (K-Wave). Every 50 to 60 years we enter a deflationary period, which follows four or five decades of inflation. Every college freshman studying economics learns this cycle in Economics 101. See Figure 1.

This chart coincides with illiquidity in the banking system. When banks get totally "loaned out," as today, the cycle has peaked, and when bank liquidity is greatest, the cycle bottoms. This is because the K-Wave is based on *debt*. Every several decades all entities assume levels of debt that can finally no longer be serviced, even during a moderate economic downturn. Debt defaults then create deflations that cleanse the system. This wave has been repeating itself for centuries.

❖ The Harmony of Business Cycles ❖

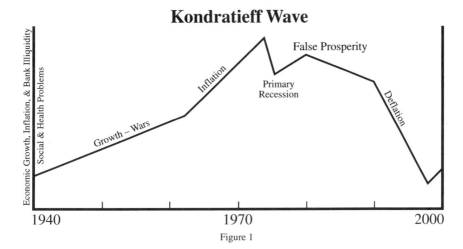

Figure 1

It should be noted there are four phases in each long wave. The first phase represents growth. Money is plentiful and cheap, and commerce flourishes. As countries compete for trade, this is also the period that produces the most wars. Yes, the economic cycle also causes most conflicts. If the perpetrating country has experienced a hyperinflation, wars will occur early in this phase. If not, most wars will occur in the next phase.

A growing economy, and particularly armed conflicts, consume capital. Money is normally "printed" to foot the bill. This is the inflation phase, and its end marks the peak of the long cycle.

A major "primary recession" then occurs. This normally marks a peak in the inflation rate. Production nears over-production. This commences the third phase—a period of "false prosperity." Inflation means debt of some type. All entities struggle with this debt load and money becomes very expensive. The inflation rate finally falls. Wars are notoriously absent during this and the next phase.

The final phase is deflation—debt liquidation. You see a natural progression here, spring, summer, fall, and winter. And this cycle, like any other, then repeats itself anew.

In his book *The Long Wave*, that includes the original translated paper by Kondratieff from the 1920s, Julian M. Snyder points out the following:

> "In 1974, exactly 54 years after the commodities explosion and collapse of 1920, another peaking and collapse occurred. Students of economic history noted with some astonishment that the previous such peak had taken place exactly 54 years before in 1866 and an almost identical phenomenon had begun 54 years earlier still in 1812...A 54 year cycle can be found in the history of agricultural prices going as far back as the year 1260; the Mayans in Central America held festivals to ward off a calamity that occurred in a 54 year cycle..."

❖ *The Harmony of Business Cycles* ❖

Please note from Figure 1 that this is not only an economic cycle, but also defines *health and social trends*. When we are the most extended economically, we are also reaching the worst periods of health problems and social dysfunction. There is no doubt where we are today. The condition of our health is absolutely terrible. It seems everything, including white mice, is serving as a catalyst to produce cancer, and ecologically we are destroying our world and animal friends. AIDS is taking lives at an exponential rate. We are killing ourselves with stress, alcohol, and nicotine.

Socially, we are in terrible shape. Divorce is epidemic, families are estranged. Millions are attending Twelve-Step meetings to deal with addictions and confusing childhoods. Physical and sexual abuse is so common it doesn't even make the front pages of the newspaper. Amidst one of the most extended economic expansions of the century we have millions of homeless. Materialism has produced the "me generation." "I don't care about you; give me my share and give it to me now."

That's the bad news. The good news is we are as sick in social and health terms as we will be for the next forty years. This is also true financially. But unlike the advent of healthier and more conservative social and health trends, as we start removing the excesses in debt, pain will be incurred. Our society and government are severely addicted to credit. And like the heroin addict who goes cold turkey, the withdrawal pains from debt will not be pleasant for those owing money. The same holds true for business owners who depend on sales originating from borrowed money.

The easiest way to see how the Kondratieff Wave works is by reviewing the last complete cycle. The next few pages describe this process. Today we are in the same phase as the late 20s or early 30s. We see major similarities between now and the pre-crash days of 1929:

- Banks are again fully loaned out
- Major international arguments over trade
- Enormous levels of debt

- An overheated stock or real estate market
- A long period of inflation/monetary abuse

In fact, we're in worse shape now than in 1929. America is today incurring huge trade deficits. In 1929 we experienced *trade surpluses*. Our government is now running chronic and massive budget deficits. In 1929 we had *budget surpluses*. Being the world's largest debtor country would have been inconceivable in 1929.

In order to zero in on where the investment explosions will occur over the next four years we only have to determine *where the most debt is located*. In 1929 the greatest debt was in the stock market. The stock market did not cause the depression, it was simply the investment attracting the most debt. Stock margin requirements were only 10%. This means you could buy $1000 of stock with only $100, borrowing the rest. And everyone owned stock. We've all heard stories of prominent businessmen who got out of the market when their shoe shine boys started telling them which equities to buy. Remember, "What everyone knows in investing isn't worth knowing." The ensuing deflation took stocks down by nearly the same percentage of their leveraging, about 90%.

At that time it wasn't unusual to put 50% down on real estate and pay off the remaining loan in five years. As a result, real estate only fell about 50%. Nevertheless, many properties were lost because people couldn't pay the taxes on real estate that was free and clear.

Today, the situation is reversed (and it's not unusual for land/real estate and stocks to alternate from one cycle to the next). Margin requirements on stocks are much more conservative today at 50%. But how many people do you know that buy stocks on margin? That's not where the most debt is located this time.

But people are still buying real estate with 10% to 20% down. Traveling salvation shows even explain how to buy real estate with 0% down. (Incidentally, most such "experts" have already fallen to bankruptcy.) Furthermore, mortgages are

❖ *The Harmony of Business Cycles* ❖

typically for thirty years. Compare the number of people you know who have bought stocks on margin to those who have bought real estate on credit. And what does everyone "know" is the best investment that cannot and will not decline in price? Where is the debt today? That's where the greatest damage will be found—in real estate. Yet because the stock market is directly dependent on the rest of the economy, stock prices will again decline massively. Furthermore, even if investors aren't borrowing heavily to buy stocks, most individual companies owe great sums of borrowed money, via bonds and commercial paper.

So in 1929 the most debt-laden and widely-held investment, the stock market, started to collapse. To pay for loans on such investments, other assets were sold. Nevertheless, huge numbers of loans defaulted. When debts go bad, money disappears from the system, just like money is added when loans are assumed (see Chapter Two).

The 1930s saw outright deflation as prices and wages fell, with the Consumer Price Index turning negative. Remember that this was only the observed effect, as fewer dollars caused the value of each dollar to increase. Runs on banks caused hundreds to close and the unemployment rate reached 25%. During this period people quickly saw the effects of debt and refused to borrow or couldn't even qualify for loans. The savings rate soared as debt was shunned and people put away what they could.

This process continued in fits and starts until 1940. World War II required huge amounts of money, and new debt was issued to pay the bills. Patriotism came to the fore, as people bought war bonds. Some money was simply printed. But this new round of inflation worked...the money supply started growing and the economy began moving forward again. But spending was still low, as certain war materials were even unavailable for public consumption.

Following World War II, banks still open were full of money from more than a decade of saving. A small percentage of deposits was "loaned out." The nation was extremely liquid.

And after the pain and anguish of a massive war, people were ready to live again. Soldiers returned home to pursue educations, start families, resume jobs, buy homes and furnish them, and again enjoy the finer things of life. And their money was sitting in banks that were still open, ready to go.

Post-war business boomed as savings were again spent. America also took the lead in providing the West and the Far East with products and assisting in their rebuilding. After all, the U.S. was the *only* major country structurally untouched by the war. It was therefore natural for our country to be the dominant power worldwide for many years—politically, militarily, and economically.

Heavy spending was incurred in the 1950s due to the Korean War and massive highway construction in the U.S. But still we managed to accomplish this without incurring significantly greater government debt—because of huge trade surpluses, a booming economy, and high tax revenues.

But the situation started to change in the early 1960s. The first thing that happened was savings were exhausted. But "a little debt never hurt anyone," so borrowing again started to increase. Massive borrowing was also again necessary by Washington to pay for an expensive space race, the Vietnam War, and something instigated by a man called Lyndon Johnson. His "Great Society" instituted costly social programs we're still trying to pay for today. The stage was also being set to slip a couple notches in our level of competitiveness worldwide. Factories that were completely destroyed in Europe and Japan were fully replaced with new, modern and efficient plants.

Heavy government spending and borrowing created two important developments. We started to incur budget deficits, and money supply started to surge. More money started an incredible inflationary period. "Prices" started their upward climb (the dollar started losing value).

As inflation works its way into the economy, the price of everything never appears to rise with equal speed. It starts with those commodities in shortest supply. In the 1960s the rarest commodity was labor. The unemployment percentage was virtually nil. The 1960s was the decade of labor inflation. Workers and labor unions demanded higher wages and those demands were granted. If you entered the job market in the early 60s, you probably thought you had died and gone to heaven...or that your wonderful talents were indispensable. Much of those higher wages was spent on recreation. This was the time to invest in companies providing those products and services. For example, if your family owned a bowling alley during that period, you drove a brand new sports car. Housing was also directly affected by higher wages. Home prices started to take off.

When any owned commodity increases sharply in price, it can be used as wonderful collateral to borrow even more money from your local banker. All you had to do was produce any kind of W-2 statement, and the bank would throw money at you. Higher wages were used as collateral to set the stage for the next major wave of inflation the following decade.

But if someone or something benefited greatly, someone had to lose. Remember, wealth is not created, but only shifted from one person or enterprise to another. On the winning side we found workers, recreation companies, home prices and the real estate industry in general. On the losing side were savers and the banks. Savers received interest rates that barely covered the yearly decline in the value of the dollar as measured by the inflation rate. Adjusted for inflation, bond prices were decimated. Banks committed themselves to loans of some 30 years' duration at interest rates that would actually become less than the inflation rate itself.

Government spending rocketed even higher in the 1970s on the heels of pork barrel legislation, defense spending, and even more social programs. Third-world countries received massive loans that could never be repaid. Government debt climbed so high that interest alone became one of our largest budget items. On the consumer side, wages had created the collateral for a new and massive wave of borrowing in the

1970s. As debt reached record levels the money supply soared and the value of the dollar plummeted.

What were the rarest items that climbed in "price" the most quickly? The 1970s was the decade of asset inflation. This included homes, manufactured products, or commodities of virtually any type. But if real estate, commodities, and manufactured goods were the winners, who were the losers? Again it was savers and banks, for the exact same reasons as before. Bond prices, in real dollars adjusted for inflation, and bondholders also suffered anew.

1974 was a landmark year. The rate of change in the inflation rate reached a very high level. Our warring years were finally over during this long wave, after we pulled out of Vietnam. Americans ejected both their President and Vice-President. A bone-crushing recession followed. The 1970s also again saw the last vestiges of a monetary gold standard disappear, and Americans could again legally own gold. (The "anchor" on our government's ability to print money was cut loose.) The creation rate of new government agencies and economic laws peaked in that decade.

Many believe 1974 was the top of the K-Wave, that the recession that immediately followed was the "primary recession" identified in all long waves, and that the period following has simply been the period of "false prosperity" only masked by inflation. In other words, the health of our economy has declined in real terms ever since 1974, although we have yet to enter the most rapid down phase. Average wages, adjusted for inflation, have fallen 20% since this key year.

Nevertheless, demand for assets in the 1970s seemed insatiable. Farmers, manufacturers, and mines couldn't produce the stuff fast enough. Huge, expensive farm equipment was purchased to speed production and new ground was bought and planted; manufacturers built new factories and warehouses to deal with the never-ending cries for more; new mines were opened worldwide demanding the latest and largest of new equipment to increase production. All this required

❖ *The Harmony of Business Cycles* ❖

even more loans, and current and projected sales certainly qualified such borrowing. The "setup" was established for companies, farmers, and many others, as huge monthly debt payments were incurred.

But something interesting happened in 1980-1982. All that increased production capability created such quantities of products that supply finally exceeded demand. We reached what is called a clearing price. A glut was present. Prices of commodities bounced higher in 1980 in their last gasp rise before starting a long decline. Someone else was hard at work during the same period. Inflation was becoming socially unacceptable, so in 1980 the Federal Reserve Bank slammed on the brakes hard. Interest rates were driven to incredibly high levels to halt inflation. And its back was broken. This produced a credit crunch when numerous entities borrowed money just to stay alive. The result was a nasty recession. In fact, we experienced two recessions within a four-year period. In boxing terms the economy had received another crippling body blow, following that of 1975, and was barely standing.

Since 1975 we had been firmly entrenched in the exhaust phase, the period of "false prosperity." So in the fall of 1982, when the Fed again inflated, something bizarre occurred.

The bookstores were filled with books on how to make inflation work for you. Gold investors were salivating at the next run higher that would produce $2000/ounce gold, coupled with $200/ounce silver. Every professional investor knew that it would only take about eighteen months for the new money to work its way into the system and for inflation to truly soar. And everything started falling into place. Interest rates first fell dramatically and bond prices took off. The stock market, true to fashion, began a meteoric rise. And in 18 months the inflation rate...well, nothing happened. Gold and silver investors were shocked. What was happening? Where was all that new money, created by new debt, going? If the money supply was again surging, what was appreciating in price? Any guesses?

The final "price inflation" was in financial assets, creating a speculative stock market bubble which would first be pricked in October, 1987. The newest debt was in corporate America. Company after company was devoured by other companies, on the heels of low-grade "junk" bonds. Like the animal that chews off its foot in a trap to save itself, target companies often incurred huge levels of debt simply to become a less palatable meal for other animals. Junk bonds became the rage. Government debt soared by trillions, as truckloads of new treasury bonds and treasury bills went to market. But consumers also kept borrowing and buying real estate. Credit card debt continued to soar.

Every long wave sees a late massive increase in stock prices. Once the back of inflation is broken, wages and material prices moderate, and business profits firm. So stocks are bid much higher, as investors expect a "soft landing."

So who were the winners during the 1980s? Finally savers were starting to be compensated. Interest rates were deregulated, and more than covered the inflation rate, though not by much. Stock investors were also winners. Banks started to benefit, as some long-term loans had been written at rates well in excess of a much lower inflation rate. Unfortunately, more and more of those loans were becoming uncollectable. So the secret was to own safe debt or stocks that didn't blow up in your face.

The losers of the 1980s were debtors. Interest on debt started eating them alive. More personal and company bankruptcies occurred...from major airline companies to brokerage firms. From John Connally to the Hunt family. Among the losers were many investors in the long-past winners of yesteryear. Truckloads of investors in oil, gas, and real estate partnerships first saw the value of their investments fall, and then found their money couldn't even be accessed. State by state, increasing numbers of people saw real estate stop appreciating, begin to fall, or start to plummet.

With the economy barely standing, it will take little to trigger the next deflation. A recession will occur, and most people

❖ *The Harmony of Business Cycles* ❖

will expect another great economic recovery. Optimistic expectations might even create a measurable bounce in the economy. But recessionary recovery will be aborted as we repeat a great debt liquidation that most people will call a major depression.

What will happen next? What will be the next rare item in the economy? The value of one commodity in particular has already started to shine. That commodity is cash. Look around you carefully. Those aren't dollar bills in the hands of your neighbors and co-workers. They're pieces of paper that promise repayment of loans. The winners of the next 10 years will be people who have safe cash to buy devastated assets, or who can lend others money. But whether the borrower is the federal government or your cousin, make sure they will be able to repay the loan.

Much of that which was put up for collateral over the last three decades will be sold to raise cash and repay loans. As assets hit the market in full force, their prices will plummet. We are now entering a period of debt liquidation and deflation. In a short period of time the Consumer Price Index will turn negative.

Debt is one addiction that will be removed from you, whether you like it or not. And there are only three things you can do with debt: Pay it off, default on it, or renegotiate it. Many loans will be negotiated and renegotiated, perhaps several times. This is because the creditor probably doesn't want to write it off altogether, and what was purchased with the loan might have little value whatsoever. A creditor will often be forced to get what little he can.

In summary, we can use the Kondratieff Cycle to come within several years of predicting massive economic change. Leading up to the current period, similarities between the 1920s and the 1980s are simply astounding:

- Certainty that the government can "avert crisis"
- A tremendous rise in the stock market

- Interest allowed on checking accounts (more expensive money, meaning riskier loans by banks)
- Huge margin debt and borrowing (previously stocks, now real estate)
- Rising trade disputes
- Much lower inflation compared to the prior decade
- Low regulation, even deregulation
- Low money supply growth
- High merger activity
- Record auto profits during the decade
- High tech growth
- Mediocre/falling bank profits
- Farm crisis
- Falling energy prices
- Republican President (pro-business)
- Big tax cuts
- Prohibition (was alcohol, now drugs)
- A sharp rise in crime
- Economists convinced depression impossible

These are the amazing similarities. Today there are four major differences, however. In the 1920s the U.S. was enjoying the prosperity and the trade advantages. Today that role has shifted to Japan. As mentioned earlier, the U.S. now has massive trade deficits—in the 1920s we experienced trade surpluses. We now have massive, chronic budget deficits—in the 1920s we had budget surpluses. And today America is the world's largest debtor country. In other words, we're in much worse shape now than during the same phase of the prior cycle.

Some like Ravi Batra, *The Great Depression of 1990*, believe this cycle is comprised of two 30-year periods. He also pinpoints the 1970s as a decade of peaking inflation and economic legislation. As mentioned earlier, he also believes major economic declines occur when the most wealth is located in the fewest hands. We are now attacking the record levels of 1929 in this respect.

❖ *The Harmony of Business Cycles* ❖

This latter factor is important. Wealthy people take greater risks with their investments. And late in a cycle even the banks join in the same game. Eventually the public also dives into those same markets. But the individual, seeking to become another Donald Trump, cannot as easily withstand the inevitable decline. They have less or no clout with major creditors for their leveraged investments based on debt. Even most banks, as they become totally loaned out, experience enormous difficulty as their investments decline in value and borrowers default on loans.

Batra also defines the difference between recessions and depressions: Recessions are caused by a drop in consumer demand (and often aggravated by higher interest rates). Depressions are recessions accompanied by failures in the financial community. Are financial institutions healthy today? In the U.S., the savings and loan mess has now been largely resolved, at enormous taxpayer expense. America's banks have done well in the most recent expansion, but will encounter unfathomable problems as the stock and real estate markets begin their collapse, and credit card defaults mount. More importantly worldwide, however, Japan's banks are the world's largest and conduct business around the globe. These institutions are already in very serious trouble and have billions in bad loans. This is primarily due to loans within their stock and real estate markets, which have already declined in price by 50%.

Batra concludes that history dictates if we escape a depression during one 30-year cycle, which we did, the following economic decline produces a depression. Batra predicted the latter, beginning in 1990. Interestingly, it was January of 1990 that the Japanese stock market started a major plunge of more than 50%. Japanese and California real estate also began a major decline in the same year.

Elliott Wave Theory correctly predicted the appreciation of the stock market during the 1980s, and is now forecasting major problems. Robert Prechter is the leading figure in Elliott Wave. He points out another phenomenal development. A 50/60 year period is called a Supercycle using Elliott Wave. Prechter explains that we are now completing a Grand Supercycle, with a periodicity of 200 years. This makes sense if one considers we are now in much worse financial shape than in 1929. Many will even say we're now completing a 2000 year cycle.

All these factors considered, the current financial deflation began in 1990. By 1998, debt will have been removed from the system, markets will start to bottom out, and we will commence a new, clean rebirth economically, politically, and morally.

Of one thing I'm quite confident. In the next four years we will see quantum change, and perhaps the most exciting period in the written history of the world. This is no time to cling to old personal belief systems. Simply get in the flow of events, whether it be economic, social, or spiritual. Not doing so will be akin to trying to swim up a waterfall.

The Recession Cycle

The deflation cycle helps us predict rare quantum change. But it doesn't even tell us whether we should be buying stocks, bonds, or CDs in a specific year, let alone tomorrow. It turns out we can get much closer to predicting the next year by using what is called the 7-year cycle. Such a period might be more familiar if we called it the recession cycle. Every 6-10 years we experience a recession. Figure 2 describes how stocks, bonds, and gold respond within a typical recession cycle. Real estate prices tend to move in a manner similar to the stock market for these shorter cycles.

Let's walk through such a period. Assume we're in the throes of a recession. So the Federal Reserve Board decides to engineer another expansion. Using the tools described in Chapter Two the FRB influences a sharp drop in interest rates by lowering the Discount Rate and buying treasury securities.

The first thing to happen is bond prices start to rise as interest rates fall. Because the inflation rate is still declining due to the recession, gold continues to fall.

❖ *The Harmony of Business Cycles* ❖

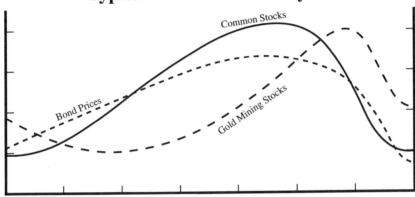

Figure 2

The stock market then takes off. Lower interest rates are good for stocks for various reasons. First, companies now operate on very high levels of borrowed money, so lower rates allow them to refinance at lower costs. But more importantly, lower interest rates mean customers will be more tempted to borrow money and buy what companies sell. As the economy improves, more people will go back to work, increasing consumption even further. So now we have two bull markets in force, bonds and stocks.

It generally takes about eighteen months for new money to work its way through the system and to be reflected in the prices of commodities, manufactured goods, services, and wages. So roughly 1 1/2 years from the initial stimulation, the Consumer Price Index bottoms out and again starts to rise. Most people buy gold as an inflation hedge, so the prices of gold and stocks of gold mining companies start rising.

Inflation accelerates more. Because this factor is an important consideration in free market interest rates, bonds finally start to top out after a few years as interest rates stop declining. As the business of companies is healthy, more corporate bonds must be issued for expansion. High levels of borrowing tend to increase some interest rates, and bond prices start to turn down. The most rapid phase of higher stock prices has also been achieved. But gold and gold mining stocks continue higher.

Eventually the economy gets too "hot" and inflation reaches unacceptable levels. It's time to slow things down and again reduce inflation. The Federal Reserve Bank starts increasing bank interest rates by increasing the Discount Rate and soaking up money in the banking system by selling treasury securities. Bond prices start to fall in earnest as interest rates rise.

There can be a delay, but stock prices soon start to decline. Higher interest rates create greater borrowing costs for companies, and also reduces borrowing and spending by customers. There is also a delay of many months between the time

❖ *The Harmony of Business Cycles* ❖

the Fed hits the brakes and inflation starts to ebb. So gold and gold mining stocks continue to rise.

But eventually inflation starts to fall as borrowing dries up and less money in the system reduces product demand and price pressures. The prices of gold-related investments start to decline. The next recession begins, and the economy will not grow again until the next wave of new inflation by the Fed.

It should be noted these are normal cycles that would occur with or without the Fed. The latter entity simply increases the magnitude of economic swings.

I've always found it amazing that so few businesses, particularly small businesses, use this recession cycle for planning purposes. But the people most often holding the bag are those individuals starting new businesses, right before the next recession. This obviously contributes heavily to the astronomical 90% failure rate of new ventures. There is an obvious reason why most new concerns are started at the most inopportune time...it simply takes some capital to get started. This money is diligently accumulated for a period of four or five years by working for another company. Once enough has been set aside, our new entrepreneur carefully watches the economy to pick the best time to get started. When he or she sees high demand for their product in the marketplace, they dive into the water. Of course what's happening is our new entrepreneurs are observing the "sweet spot" of the expansion. It usually takes at least a year to get fully established and start attracting some customers. Just as the next recession begins.

Business owners should follow, quite literally, what professional investors already know. You obtain maximum price for a business by selling the firm when the economy hits its 7-year "sweet spot." (This is also the most propitious time to sell real estate, stocks, and other assets except gold, if you want top price.) The professional investor or business broker will then buy a business or company at the depths of the recession, right before the next stimulation by the Fed. It might even be the same business you sold two years prior. Or this might enable you to "save" those Wrong Way Corrigans who by now are panicking in their new business as their capital nears zero and bills continue to come in. One can obtain such businesses for peanuts. Even if you need office furniture or equipment for a new or refurbished venture, this is exactly when tons of such items are available for a song, if you can swallow your pride and buy used instead of new.

Using the 7-year cycle allows you to vastly improve your investment timing. You can easily come within a year of buying stocks, bonds, and gold at their lows and selling at their highs. By knowing what signs to look for, and with some experience, one can come within months of perfect buys and sells. With lower inflation, however, the last 7-year cycle is modified somewhat during the last stage of the long cycle. This affects gold prices in particular. More on this later.

So use 50/60 year cycles to know where you are in the inflation/deflation cycle; to predict which investments will do best during that phase of the cycle; and to determine whether you should be accumulating debt or getting out of debt as soon as possible.

Use the 7-year cycle to get an even better idea of when you should actually be buying or selling stocks, bonds, and gold. There will be a period of about one year very late in such typical cycles that all three will be declining. This is when you sit on safe and liquid cash positions, and take your long vacations.

But this still doesn't tell us what day to buy or sell. This final touch will be discussed in Chapter Seven.

Causes of Deflation and Recession Cycles

If you're like me, however, you don't easily accept new concepts about very important things at face value. In other words, you will refuse to lend much credence to things like deflation and recession cycles unless you can see some reason why they occur. I followed the same thought process, and will

❖ *The Harmony of Business Cycles* ❖

now share some of what I learned that causes these waves.

First, the deflation cycle. Generational effects go far in explaining why we do the same stupid things every five or six decades. Take, for example, our major decision-makers in 1929. The leaders of major corporations and our government itself tend to be in their late 50s and 60s. Once the economy fell apart the last time, it was clearly obvious to many such people how debt caused the collapse, and how the situation developed. Were they around in 1962 when we started the massive inflation of the last three decades? Not unless they lived to be 90-100 years old. Those who could warn us of what we were doing were simply no longer with us. That wisdom, that direct experience, was simply gone.

The same applies to family practices. We will often imitate the characteristics, habits, and choices of our parents, but not be able to relate to those of our grandparents. In order to profit from what our parents learned by direct experience, in terms of deflations and stock market crashes, it's necessary that our parents lived the experiences of 1929 and the 1930s as aware adults. This means our parents must still be alive today, which would now make them 85 years old. How many such people are still alive today, and still alert and cogent enough, to show us how to benefit from, and not fall victim to, the changes they experienced? Very few. Nevertheless, to this day such people still, after all that time, avoid debt like the plague.

Planetary relationships greatly influence cyclical change. A research project at RCA proved that planetary configurations could be used to predict radio wave interference. And if the human mind/body are electrochemical in nature, we might expect to be similarly influenced. Many people totally reject most aspects of what is called astrology. But you might be interested to know that even this pursuit is calling for massive change.

Diane Lancaster of Lancaster and Associates of Boulder, CO, is a business analyst and visionary who has written and lectured extensively on the economic times ahead, the spiritual dimensions of entrepreneurship and the redistribution of power and wealth. She has consulted several Fortune 500 companies as well as entrepreneurs and inventors. Her current astrological observations:

"Government deceit involving debt is what the placement of the planet Pluto in the United States' natal chart will bring out in the last half of the decade. Pluto will also oversee massive and dramatic upheaval and overhaul in relation to values, resources and the redistribution of power and wealth.

Glimpses of the components of the series of economic crises that lie ahead will be evidenced by whatever issues are in the spotlight the fall of 1995. That is the period the planet Uranus, moving through the heavens, conjoins Pluto's position in the United States chart. Uranus brings abrupt awareness to economic issues that, according to Pluto, absolutely must be addressed and transformed.

Uranus will hover around the United States Pluto all of 1995, relentlessly insisting that whatever it has illuminated be addressed. And to guarantee its message is not ignored, Uranus will then defer to the planet Neptune which conjoins the United States Pluto just as Uranus moves away. By January 1996, therefore, Neptune will be at work dissolving the barriers to truth; and Neptune remains on duty in that capacity until the end of 1998.

The Uranus/Neptune/Pluto truths are related to fiscal mismanagement, incompetency, abuse of power, denial and deceit. Uranus produces sudden awareness. Neptune clouds and dissolves. Pluto signifies issues of huge proportion.

Together they will reveal massive, cumulative underlying conditions that have been denied. For example, the stock market has climbed to record highs because of displaced wealth. Stagnant wages and other squeezes on the lower economic levels have pushed money to the top, creating the *appearance* of new wealth and economic stability...but not sustainable wealth. Neptune creates the illusion of wealth and stability; Uranus will eventually abruptly reveal the irreversible consequences; and Pluto will ensure that the markets, the government, and all the financial institutions that have perpetuated this false security lose both the power and the wealth that have aggregated in this manner.

These Plutonian issues are also connected to a reality ignored: That patently applying macroeconomic models derived from past decades to the current, unprecedented situation of trillions of dollars of debt has produced impotent fiscal strategies and myopic monetary policies.

Progressively weakened from such unsound helmsmanship, the United States economy (and the global economy, as a result) will experience bouts of inflation, recession, stagflation and ultimately, depression.

In the face of such consequences and crises, this nation's economic leadership will be wrested from the political arena and vested in an aggregate of individuals and expertise whose responsibility for austere, accountable stewardship of the economic power and resources of this nation will be directed toward the greatest good for the greatest number."

Some people say earth shifts, sunspot activity, and, or major weather cycles also have similar periodicity. We are now experiencing some of the strongest weather in memory, including earthquakes, hinting of a possible return to the weather-related disasters during the last depression. I haven't thoroughly researched the subjects, because of an even more conclusive item I'll mention in a few pages. But these are some of the causes, effects, and observations my research has uncovered on the Kondratieff Wave.

Seven-year waves are more quickly accepted by virtually anyone, simply because they occur more often, and because we've personally experienced so many of them. There is no doubt that physically and psychologically our minds and bodies are governed by 7-year cycles. The body also renews its skin every 7 years. As I look back on my own life, dramatic changes have occurred every 7 years. And I'm not talking about minor events, but changes where you can almost hear one door slam shut and another open. My move overseas, my quitting employment with a multinational company and the starting of my own advisory business, and my entry into

Twelve Step were separated by exactly 7 years. Having published a monthly investment newsletter for a period, it wasn't until one year after it was discontinued that I realized I had written the letter for...well, guess how many years.

If you take the average number of years divorced people were married, you obtain 7 years. I've made a bit of a game of asking divorced acquaintances how long they were married. Answers are typically 7 years or 13 years. (I don't know why it might be 13 instead of two periods totaling 14.) Yes, there is something to the "seven year itch."

Until very recently, what were the number of years prevailing in bankruptcy law? We've already stated that the 50/60 year cycle is firmly based on debt. Every 7 years we simply see a natural minor correction attempt to adjust the level of debt.

Seven is the lucky number. There are 7 days in a week. There are 7 energy centers (chakras) in the body. The list goes on and on. Once aware of such things, you will be amazed at how often the number presents itself. During one of my seminars I asked the audience if the number seven meant anything to them. One young lady raised her hand and said "Seven is God's number."

In reality, the number 3 numerologically represents God, and 4 is the number of man. Add the two and we get the combined realm of the two working together—7.

The latter is a good introduction to the oldest reference to these cycles my research has uncovered. A few years back I was discussing finance and investment cycles with a doctor friend. When I mentioned these two cycles he thought for a minute and said: "You know, I have a friend who's an avid student of *The Bible*, and he's described the same cycles." A few days later I talked to his friend. And I now refer you to Leviticus 25, verses 4-17:

> But in the seventh year there shall be a Sabbath to the land, of the resting of the Lord: thou shalt not sow thy field, nor prune thy vineyard...

❖ *The Harmony of Business Cycles* ❖

> ...for it is a year of rest to the land:
>
> ...Thou shalt also number to thee seven weeks of years, that is to say, seven times seven, which together make forty-nine years: And thou shalt sound the trumpet in the seventh month, the tenth day of the month, in the time of the expiation in all your land. And thou shalt sanctify the fiftieth year, and shalt proclaim remission to all the inhabitants of thy land: for it is the Year of Jubilee. Every man shall return to his possessions, and every one shall go back to his former family:
>
> ...When thou shalt sell any thing to thy neighbor, or shalt buy of him; grieve not thy brother: but thou shalt buy of him according to the number of years from the jubilee.
>
> ...The more years remain after the jubilee, the more shall the price increase: and the less time is counted, so much the less shall the purchase cost.

Every 7 days we rest. Every 7 years we rest from the fruits of our labor. Every 50 years we have forgiveness of debt as man returns to his possessions and is reunited with his family. Incredibly enough, inflation is also described. Prices rise slowly following a deflation, and as time proceeds, prices rise more quickly, until the next jubilee.

But how might one explain the fact that current cycles tend to occur in somewhat longer periods, for example, something in excess of 50 and 7 years? This is what I call the "workout period." We are destined to cleanse the system every 50 years, and to a smaller degree, every 7 years. But if debt is not immediately forgiven at the end of such periods, we must work out the excess over a few years. This simply extends such periods. Seven-year cycles can reach 10 years in length. The long wave averages 54 years peak to peak. The years separating other like events, however, can be extended by one 7 year cycle to make 61 years. (Note that 1990 is the sum of 1929 and 61.) In 1990 the stock market and commercial real estate market of the world's major economic power, Japan, began a crushing decline that has already forced both 50% lower. That same year saw the advent of sharply lower real estate prices in the overheated California market, and some commercial real estate has been purchased for 15% of current construction costs. This is only the beginning.

So these long and intermediate cycles have been in place for at least 2000 years. Depending on your religious or spiritual beliefs you are free to interpret this as biblical law or universal law. It simply "is".

My first reaction to this learning was awe. But not today. I now know that everything we can see, touch, or hear in this world is based on a wave or cycle. In 1987 I conducted a twelve-week study course called "The Masters Program." One week's assignment to the students was to come up with something—anything—which wasn't based on a wave or cycle. No one could even think of so much as a concept that the rest of the group couldn't describe in wave form. Light and sound are waves. The lonely rock is composed of nuclear particles that rotate around each other. Even a straight line, in Russian mathematics, is defined as the circumference of a circle of infinite radius. Everything, including that thing we call life, is a cycle. Everything is in harmony, and nothing is random. Randomness is only something we don't yet understand in our powerful, but often mistaken minds.

4

Evaluation

> *Before I built a wall I'd ask to know
> what I was walling in or walling out.*
> —Robert Frost

IT IS TIME TO make a fearless and searching inventory of our investments. Some might think this unnecessary, particularly if they don't have any savings or what are normally called investments. I guarantee you have investments, because we're using the generic definition. Investment represents your focus, and your concentration of beliefs, of time and of money. In fact, a close analysis of your financial investments will help you understand your emotional investments.

We will do this in two ways, first by completing your Balance Sheet. This includes your assets (or financial talents and capital), and your liabilities (your debts and expectations). If you don't know where you are, it is virtually impossible to decide where you're going and how to get there.

Next you will review your expenses. How do you spend your time and money, and how does this relate to your income? How are you doing with your cash flow, and why?

Finally we will evaluate each typical financial investment available to you today. We will review the pros and cons of each, and determine which you best avoid and which are worthy of your closer analysis. The latter will greatly simplify your life by allowing you to concentrate on and increase your understanding of the most important. And I guarantee you right now that you will be able to invest in the most appropriate with the tiniest of funds.

Balance Sheet

We are intentionally using the term balance sheet rather than net worth. This is because the latter has insane implications. Money does not determine your worth. And please think of balance sheet not in terms of accounting, but in terms of the balance in your life.

Your balance sheet is comprised of two parts. The first part is your assets. This is your immediate potential, your reserves, the gas in your tank today, your savings. The second part is your liabilities. These are your current limitations, your debts, the expectations placed on you by your creditors. Adding the two together provides your net potential.

Let's first review your assets—your immediate potential. Complete the following list. In many cases estimates will do, but be careful not to fool yourself. Be honest. This is for your benefit and growth.

For assets, enter the net amount if you were to turn each asset into cash within 60 days. For certain funds, annuities, etc., this might entail a redemption fee or early withdrawal penalty. Deduct such amounts. For real estate, enter a "quick sale" figure if you were to dispose of the property within 60 days, less estimated sales commissions and closing costs. Exclude mortgage balances and taxes due until later. For autos, enter only the amount by which current estimated value of any individual vehicle exceeds $10,000. For stocks, bonds, etc., use the last available price, again less estimated sales commissions. For limited partnerships, you might not even be able to sell your asset. In such illiquid situations enter 50% of current estimated value. If others owe you debt, enter only the amount they could repay in 60 days, unless the debtor is ex-

❖ Evaluation ❖

tremely reliable and capable of repayment. (If fully capable of repayment, why was the money borrowed?) Don't include most household or personal items except for unique collectibles devoid of enormous emotional investment. Include real market sales value (what you paid is meaningless) of such items including gold and diamond jewelry. If values are not immediately available for such things, enter 10% of the price you paid.

If you own your own business, or part of one, I suggest you enter 70 times last month's net after-tax company earnings, times your percentage ownership. Add to this a conservative estimate of the liquidation value of real assets like property and used plant and equipment, and the cash value of investments and other liquid assets, less company liabilities. Again adjust for your percentage ownership. Your accountant might be able to offer a quick rule of thumb to estimate a reasonable market value for your particular type of business, based on the profits it generates. Each business is different. The two most important considerations are to first be very conservative, and secondly, to be consistent by always using the same method to estimate a reasonable sale value.

ASSETS

$_____	Cash in Checking Accounts
_____	Savings Accounts
_____	Savings Bonds (current sales value)
_____	Money Market Funds
_____	Cash Value of Life Insurance
_____	Certificates of Deposit

_____	Market Value, Each Auto (less $10,000)
_____	Loans Due You
_____	Real Estate, Less Closing Costs
_____	Stocks (including mutual funds)
_____	Bonds (including bond mutual funds)
_____	Annuities (net on sale)
_____	Negotiable Trust Deeds
_____	Businesses Owned
_____	Other _____
_____	_____
$_____	TOTAL ASSETS

The above guidelines don't mean you will actually sell an asset, but this is a consistent way to keep track of and compare the ever-changing value of your assets. In fact, some assets can't be liquidated per se. This includes deferred compensation plans or vested amounts in Employee Investment Plans at work. But you can shift such investments into areas that make more sense, possibly within such plans. For now, simply list the values by types of investment, perhaps making a separate note identifying the amounts within such arrangements.

These are your monetary assets. You have other potentials

❖ Evaluation ❖

or talents. Next you will inventory your personal attributes, that could potentially be turned into monetary assets or income. These are of particular importance if you have limited monetary assets.

The first item is Outside Time. List the number of hours per month you could make yourself available elsewhere without incurring extra expense. For example, you might have five children underfoot. Your days might be unavailable, without paying for child care, unless grandparents, etc. are both handy and willing a few days a month. Some evenings every month might be made available if your spouse would gladly watch after the little ones.

The next item is Inside Time. List the number of hours per month you could easily arrange to spend on additional activities at home.

Finally list your other various attributes, including areas in which you're above average in experience, training (even if self-taught), special interests...anything in which you're somewhat unique. Don't forget to include special tools or equipment which could be helpful.

It's not necessary to decide how each can be applied at this time. We'll do that in Chapter Ten. We're simply taking an inventory for now. But a few examples might be helpful. Let's say friends tell you you're particularly attractive, or that you're a dancing fool. You can type sixty words a minute. Or you can tune up your own car and easily replace brakes or shocks. Your family has a computer or word processor.

After reading Chapter Ten you might decide that you want to supplement your income for a year or two. Possibilities might be to do some modeling part time, or to teach aerobics (getting in better shape at the same time). Or you could provide typing services for small businesses in your own home. You could work part time at an automotive shop or even work on friends' cars for less than it would cost at the corner shop. Now is not the time to be modest when completing your list.

PERSONAL ATTRIBUTES

Outside Time (Hours/month): _____

Inside Time (Hours/month): _____

_____

_____

_____

It's now time to list all monetary liabilities. The list is quite straightforward with two exceptions. You'll want to get some extra numbers for each.

The first is credit card debt. Complete the information below. When filled out it will help you make some early decisions. First, check those cards on which you can obtain cash advances. Next, divide item C by item B and place this percentage in E. You can now decide which cards to pay off first.

If cash flow is a current or potential problem, it's nice to know you can obtain cash advances on cards when you can't pay a truly necessary bill with plastic. In fact, one excellent rule for credit cards is if you must pay the total balance every month and can't access cash with it, leave home without it. Cut it up and get rid of it. Such cards tend to be only for pure consumption-type items anyway. Next, pay off those cards first that you can't use to access cash, starting with the one with the highest percentage from column E. This will assist cash flow.

If cash flow isn't a problem, simply pay off first those with the highest interest rates, from column D.

❖ *Evaluation* ❖

CREDIT CARD DETAIL

Issuer	Cash Adv?	(B) Bal Owed	(C) Min Mo Pmt	(D) Int Rate	(E) C/B
_____	_____	_____	_____	_____	_____
_____	_____	_____	_____	_____	_____
_____	_____	_____	_____	_____	_____
_____	_____	_____	_____	_____	_____

Total Credit Card Debt _____

The second major item involves any taxes that would be due on gains from sale of assets. You might, for example, have bought stocks or bonds at lower than current prices and still hold those investments. Taxes would be due on sale, so that amount isn't your money and must be estimated on your liabilities sheet. You will more than likely have unrealized gains on real estate. If you don't adjust for estimated taxes if sold, you'll overestimate your net assets. So estimate gains for real estate and other investments by subtracting your tax base (usually purchase price) from current market value. After estimating tax on such gains, enter the totals in item A.

LIABILITIES

$ _____ Credit Card Balances, Total

_____ Loans on Life Insurance Cash Value

_____ Balance Owed, Auto Loans

_____	Balance Owed, Other Installment Debt
_____	Accounts Payable (Exclude Mo. Bills)
_____	Loans Payable to Others
_____	Income Taxes Payable (not deducted)
_____	Property Back Taxes Payable
_____	Real Estate Mortgage Balances
_____	Est Tax, Unrealized Capital Gains (A)
_____	Brokerage Margin Accounts Owed
_____	Other Liabilities
_____	Balance, Other Loans

$_____ TOTAL LIABILITIES

Subtract TOTAL LIABILITIES from TOTAL ASSETS and you have your CURRENT NET CAPITAL. Your objective is obviously to see capital grow steadily over the years. It becomes your money scoreboard. It makes no difference how large or small your starting number is. (This approach can also be used by your kids.) Updating every six months or so will provide you with a record of your progress as you learn and apply your new and better savings and investment strategy.

❖ *Evaluation* ❖

TOTAL ASSETS $ _____

Less TOTAL LIABILITIES   _____

CURRENT NET CAPITAL $ _____

Income and Expenses

Now that you have identified your beginning reserves, we next determine your cash flow. By comparing INCOME to CURRENT EXPENSES, you can determine what is affecting your ability to add to reserves and other investment, during a unique opportunity to massively increase your capital.

Let's first determine your after-tax income. Unless you're currently retired, I suggest you include dividends and interest on your investments as additions to assets and therefore capital. It probably depends on whether you receive such amounts or have them reinvested. If you have rental properties, I suggest you treat these as you would any business, and keep a separate account for income and expenses for each property. Monthly cash flow, if received and not reinvested, would be added to monthly income.

AFTER-TAX MONTHLY INCOME

_____ Net Wages/Salary

_____ Paid Into Deferred Compensation

_____ Paid Into Company-Matched Investment

_____ Automatic Savings/Investment

_____ Net Wages/Salary, Spouse

_____ Net Business Income

_____ Investment Income (Less est tax)

_____ Retirement Income

_____ Social Security

_____ Other _____

$_____ TOTAL MONTHLY INCOME

If you own your own business, you had the option of treating business profits as income, if received, or if not received, as increases in the value of the business. The latter would be reflected as an increase in your assets.

It is now time to identify your monthly expenses. Note the term "budget" isn't used. If you are already budgeting and carefully planning your expenses, then the term is appropriate. The vast majority of Americans simply spend, so we'll use the term "expenses" for now.

People tend to have three major problems in this area. First, they spend more than they think they do. It is now important to simply identify all spending. There is no judgment here on what is good or bad. Second, any efforts to plan are confused by those bills which occur quarterly, semi-annually, or yearly. This leads to times that expenses seem to be going quite well without problems, but with little in the checking account. Then a quarterly or other non-monthly bill suddenly comes in and we must scramble to juggle that "unexpected" outgo.

Third, we find it difficult to fit one-off type expenditures into a budget: Those tires we had to replace on the car, that VCR we bought, or the washing machine repair.

❖ *Evaluation* ❖

The following accommodates these three problems. For a fearless and searching inventory, we will go back and use check records to identify payments. Don't forget to include cash withdrawals from those frustrating teller machines, or for checks written over the amount for extra cash. And certainly don't forget to check your monthly summaries of credit card purchases. You might even have other personal ways of spending. Perhaps you own your own business and occasionally write a company check for personal expenses, or simply grab something from the cash drawer. Try to identify all outgo, by category.

Get all your records together for the last year and proceed. It makes sense to do this as a family, for two reasons. First, it helps younger members of the family gain a new respect for the importance of income and budgeting. Secondly, you will encounter difficulties in identifying some outlays. What was included in that check for $150 to Sears? Was it mom's clothing, Susie's jewelry, or dad's circular saw? Or all three? By working together, you can estimate a breakdown closely enough. (A helpful work sheet follows, comments are continued.)

AVERAGE MONTHLY SPENDING PATTERNS

    HOUSING
        Mortgage/Rent $_____
        Lawn/Garden   _____
        House Repairs   _____
        Real Estate Tax   _____

    HOUSEHOLD
        New Furniture/Appliances _____
        Appliance Repairs   _____
        Purchase Misc. Items   _____

UTILITIES
    Electricity   _____
    Oil/Gas   _____
    Telephone   _____

FOOD/MISC PERSONAL   _____

CLOTHING
    Him   _____
    Her   _____
    _____   _____
    _____   _____

CASH ALLOWANCES/MISC PERSONAL
    Him   _____
    Her   _____
    _____   _____
    _____   _____

AUTOMOBILE
    Loan Payments   _____
    Gas/Oil   _____
    Repairs/Tires   _____
    Tax/License   _____

MEDICAL/DRUGS   _____

INSURANCE
    Auto   _____
    Life   _____
    Household   _____
    Medical   _____
    Disability   _____

CHARITY/CHURCH   _____

❖ *Evaluation* ❖

CHRISTMAS GIFTS   _____

MISC GIFTS   _____

ENTERTAINMENT/
RECREATION/MEALS OUT   _____

VACATIONS   _____

CLUBS/ORGANIZATIONS   _____

COLLEGE   _____

SELF-EDUCATION/
GROWTH   _____

CHILD SUPPORT   _____

SPOUSAL SUPPORT   _____

ACCOUNTANT/TAX PREP   _____

OTHER PROF FEES   _____

*INTEREST, CREDIT CARDS   _____

*OTHER LOAN REPAYMENTS_____

OTHER   _____   _____

               _____   _____

               _____   _____

AVG. MONTHLY SPENDING: $ _____

*Be careful not to record spending twice. For credit cards, it's important to record at this time *what was purchased* to determine spending patterns. Monthly repayments, however, will play an important role in a new budget. By the same token, other loan repayments, if used for consumption such as the purchase of a new stereo system, etc., should be recorded as an appliance purchase and not loan repayment.

One extreme word of caution for completing this summary: Each member of the family will enter this process with some guilt, and might even try to block the entire process. Know in advance that everyone has one or more areas in which spending is dysfunctional. This process will likely reveal those areas. On the other hand, some people are the most tightfisted imaginable when it comes to spending, and every expense is meticulously analyzed. If this is you, you have another problem, likely involving greed, lack, or fear. So let's not have any saints in the group.

It is therefore crucial for everyone, in advance, to personally agree they will not judge anyone else for any type of spending. If your review is done with this agreement going in, knowing there is nothing to hide, you are getting close to the definition of love—i.e., total acceptance. With this newly gained freedom, the process can be a lot of fun, even producing periodic, good natured laughter as each sees funny ways he spends money.

You will need some work sheets to list expenses by category. It is helpful if one records while another goes through the check record and each monthly credit card summary. This can be done very easily and quickly. If you want the greatest rewards from such a review, try to identify each item by individual. For example, instead of simply "clothing" or "auto," go for "dad's clothing" or "mom's car." This type of detail can help you make decisions later, like trading in mom's car because it's costing too much to maintain.

Three final tips: When you encounter a quarterly, semiannual, or yearly payment, note the date. It will be helpful later to anticipate those non-monthly payouts for planning purpos-

❖ Evaluation ❖

es. (Be sure to keep all work sheets.) Next, when anyone receives cash for allowances or miscellaneous items, make sure you record who received it. Also keep an eye out for items not listed on the work sheet. One rule of thumb might be to keep track of it separately if it's estimated to be more than $50 or $100 a year. Such items might be jewelry, purchases for the shop like tools, personal items, knickknacks for the house, house repairs, etc. Once you get your yearly totals for each, divide by 12 and you have your monthly average.

Once you've identified monthly spending by category, you're not finished yet. This is because you need a little additional detail in two areas.

The first is cash. You'll agree this tells us nothing. Even though we've identified how much each person received, we want to identify what was purchased. The easiest way to do this is for each person to keep a close account of all cash expenditures for a couple weeks, and/or to make a conscious effort to try to pay for virtually everything possible by check or credit card for one month to obtain a record. The result will be an excellent breakdown of areas into such things as: Lunches, snacks, coffee at work, drinks after work, parking, cigarettes, beer, etc. Try your best not to change your patterns during that period. And again remember, absolutely no self-judgment or judgment of others.

The second area is currently identified as Food and Misc. Personal, usually from the grocery store. You can buy a vast array of things in today's supermarkets, and a breakdown here too will provide riches. For one month keep all your receipts from the grocery store, which are very detailed, then break them down into major categories for each family member. Again, it is preferable to review these receipts as a family. I know this is a big budget buster for me, primarily from "Bob's Diet Pepsi" and "Bob's snacks."

You now have a virtual gold mine for evaluation. You've heard of "garbage analysis." Incredible insight can be gained on lifestyle just by analyzing one's trash. We've developed the resources to do even better, with only some records, a pencil, paper, and a little time.

Spending Review

Now that you have all the details, you're in a position to make some important observations on spending motivation. So next go through each item and decide on the possible emotional reasons for incurring each expense, as opposed to other alternatives. Again, no judgment. Only honest insight. Recall too that in this chapter you will not make any decisions to change anything. You're only trying to identify.

The following are some truthful examples of appropriate review and consideration for linking monetary outgo with the possible related emotional motivation.

Following a sincere and honest discussion of each expense item, we made the following observations:

"We decided that our primary reason for owning such an expensive home was to appear successful. Renting looked bad. There was also a control motivation. By owning our own home we would gain control over one big item, only to lose partial control over our finances. This also increased the fear associated with coming up with a substantial payment every month. There were also investment reasons. But as we look around us, home prices are dropping. We were also surprised how much it cost for house repairs and improvements.

It was amusing to determine that our costly decision to buy the new furniture was not for us. The old stuff was a lot more comfortable and created little fear of spills, and the dog could park himself wherever he wanted. We had really bought the furniture to impress people when they visited. And we don't even entertain very often! We also spent over $1000 just for things to hang on the walls, for the same reason.

I decided that phone calls to my parents could be sharply cut. I usually called because I hadn't communicated with them in several weeks, felt guilty, and simply picked up the phone. A nice letter every few weeks would save almost $200 a year!

❖ *Evaluation* ❖

John was surprised to see we were spending almost $70 a month at Safeway just for his Diet Coke, and almost $40 a month for his coffee at work. He decided he was for some reason pretty addictive/compulsive in this area. He said if he could simply become appropriate with his Coke and coffee consumption (and really could turn $1 into $30 over the next few years), only one year's savings and investment from that area alone would be worth $25,000 after 1998. I also noticed I was spending a lot on cosmetics, and had dribs and drabs of everything possible. I'm going to carefully shop in the future, buy less, and treat myself to the best without spending more.

We found that Susie and I spent a lot on clothing, but have many clothes we never wear. By shopping more carefully we could find things we really loved to wear, treat dad to a new suit (he never buys himself anything) and still save over $500 a year.

We were absolutely shocked how much we spent on lunches—John at work, and me popping into a fast food place when running around. We thought it would be fun to meet for a really nice lobster lunch every Wednesday with the savings we could make in this area, and still have a lot left over. They have a microwave in John's office now, and they have some neat less-expensive prepackaged lunches you can now buy at the grocery store for work.

We spend more than necessary on meals at home. Because I'm busy, I often throw something already prepared into the microwave. And those ready-to-eat meals are really expensive. Susie said she'd be glad to prepare some of the meals and even John said there are some basic dishes he would be willing to occasionally fix to help out too.

I knew I spent a lot on smoking. Frankly, I was a little afraid the rest of the family would come down on me for that. They didn't. I actually cried during one of our discussions, because John and Susie were so understanding and didn't judge me. It was a wonderful, joyful, and freeing feeling that they accepted it. And I told them so. The potential savings here are also great, and I think I'll check out some Smokers Anonymous meetings.

Maybe John is getting a bit ahead of things, but he's already obtained some cheaper insurance quotes on almost all our insurance.

We spend a lot for Christmas, birthdays, and other special occasions. We decided there was a lot of people-pleasing going on here. We also observed that we seldom really love and use what we receive. By more closely determining what people would really enjoy, we could spend a lot less and still be more effective givers.

We decided we probably weren't spending enough on self-growth.

John kills himself with our taxes every year, and doesn't use an accountant. He felt this was a control issue, and an attempt to prove to us and himself he could do it. By using an accountant he would free himself, and it would probably result in enough new tax breaks to more than pay for the service.

We spend a lot each year, just on credit card debt. We could easily plan our purchases a little and pay cash. We felt all of us were a little compulsive in having things now, and often buy things we didn't truly need, just because the plastic was handy.

The above are wonderful examples of what can be learned from such a review. This particular family was getting a bit ahead of themselves by already making plans to change

❖ *Evaluation* ❖

spending, but they've gained enormous insight. This guarantees wonderful growth in Chapter Five, when a new target budget is constructed.

But don't get stuck in all the nickels and dimes and forget the big picture. We are first evaluating our current capital: What we now have available for investment and which investments we're currently using. A nice level of reserves, however, is only half the equation.

The second important part is our cash flow, determined by subtracting our spending from our income:

MONTHLY INCOME   _____

AVERAGE MONTHLY   −
SPENDING   _____

_____

MONTHLY CASH FLOW   _____

Cash flow, the positive difference, is our major engine for adding to capital and investment. We will also be discussing ways to add a couple additional pumps to this engine, and maybe throw on a turbocharger as well. But if we're spending everything we make and don't do anything about it, we're totally at the mercy of economic change, and destroying our opportunity for true financial success, during a period that offers the best opportunity for doing so.

Evaluation of Investments

When I first became a professional investment adviser, I took a hard look at economic change, and one thing was obvious. Massive change was approaching at high speed. Which investments would be the most appropriate during this period of quantum change and rapidly-growing risk?

I decided it was necessary to establish a test to determine

which investments would be most appropriate. I used three qualifiers. Each investment would more likely survive the massive change at hand if it could be rated *above average* for all three of the following:

> **SAFETY** - Low danger of default.
>
> **REAL GROWTH POTENTIAL** - The degree of monetary return possible, after taxes and after inflation. Return must also sufficiently compensate for risk.
>
> **LIQUIDITY** - The speed and ease by which one can buy or sell an investment.

Let's discuss the specifics and importance of each. Safety is often confused with price volatility. An investment can change quickly and/or greatly in price, but still be among the safest. You are perfectly free to avoid a certain type of security because you don't feel comfortable with such volatility. Be aware, however, that your reasoning has nothing to do with safety. Also be clear that any time you place your money with someone else, you're investing. Can the individual, the financial institution, or underlying security fulfill its promise and return your money without defaulting? This is the essence of safety.

You would be amazed at how low the Real Growth Potential is for many investments you're currently employing. You must first subtract the taxes you pay from interest or capital gains. Next, multiply the inflation rate percentage by the value of your original investment. You lose this amount every year, as the purchasing power of the dollar falls. (When you get your money back it buys less.) Only after these adjustments will you be working with true numbers for calculating real return. Go back and review the examples in Chapter Two under "Adjusting for Inflation."

After this adjustment, real return must be compared to

❖ *Evaluation* ❖

risk. Professional gamblers would probably best understand amount invested, potential return, and risk. Would they be interested in a real return of less than 2% if risk (danger of losing everything) were even 5%? Or would it make more sense to invest in something with a 20% potential of real return and a risk of 5%? Real return must always be greater than risk.

Liquidity is also critical. How easily and quickly can you buy or, more importantly, sell an investment? This is important because you don't know what emergency might develop, requiring that you access those funds. Safety might also fall unexpectedly after your purchase, or the price might start to decline. And few can anticipate what will happen over the next six months or a year, let alone imagine the massive change that will occur over the next four years. I currently recommend no investment that cannot be sold within twenty-four hours.

But there is also a second component to liquidity. Even if one's investment can be sold very quickly, there can be substantial psychological factors detracting from liquidity. Such liquidity problems are most often the result of commissions and early withdrawal penalties. If you've paid 8.5% for the privilege of buying certain mutual funds, or paid only a 2% commission to buy a stock, you might procrastinate much too long to prevent "losing" that fee...as prices continue to decline while you deliberate. I can clearly envision millions of people who will read the front page of their local newspapers daily about failing banks or savings and loans, and still be unable to act. "Should I forgo 2-3 months of interest as an early withdrawal penalty on my certificate of deposit, or risk repayment delays or possible loss?" Redemption fees are common for many mutual funds, and virtually the rule for annuities. The best way to avoid liquidity problems of a psychological nature is to never buy any investment that involves purchase commissions, sales commissions, front-end loads, redemption fees, or early withdrawal penalties of any kind. Place as few obstacles as possible between your decision to sell, and your ability to get your money back immediately.

So we only want to put our money into investments that have above average Safety, *and* above average Real Growth Potential, *and* above average Liquidity. To assist in doing this, I've evaluated all typical investments for each factor. Mutual funds are available for most of these investments. If the underlying security is acceptable, this is followed by a description of such a mutual fund. If not, those mutual funds are not discussed, unless they are of particular interest in our new investment strategy. Let's discuss how each investment fares, and whether it passes the test. We will rate each Pass, Fail, or Consider.

CERTIFICATES OF DEPOSIT Safety is only average. With the growing banking, savings and loan, and credit union crisis, rude surprises will quickly become the rule. From anxious delays in repayment, to possible default. The U.S. Government will soon realize it can't hope to fully guarantee all deposits up to $100,000, and I predict they will lower deposit guarantees first to $10,000 to $20,000, and possibly lower at a later date. Real Growth Potential is poor. Interest barely covers inflation and any taxes on interest. Value of principal cannot grow. Liquidity is poor. Early withdrawal fees are charged, and I've never seen a CD (check the fine print) for which the financial institution couldn't refuse the granting of early withdrawal, at their option, requiring the investor to wait until maturity. FAIL

MONEY MARKET FUNDS Safety is below average. Some 95% of all money market funds primarily buy commercial paper and CDs. Also included are bankers' acceptances and often government agency paper, treasury bills, and overseas paper. These typical money funds average 60% commercial paper, which are short-term unsecured corporate IOUs (in effect, tomorrow's short-term "junk bonds"). Defaults in commercial paper are rising ominously. Real growth potential is poor. Liquidity is excellent, usually with check writing privileges, provided the value and/or safety of underlying securities is maintained. FAIL

❖ Evaluation ❖

SAVINGS BONDS Safety is very high, as these securities would probably be the last the federal government would allow to default. Real growth potential is below average, due to low interest rates when compared to inflation and taxes. Liquidity is below average because of the need to handle sales personally, and partial loss of interest upon early redemption. FAIL

TREASURY BILLS These direct obligations of the federal government, with maturities of up to one year, are the safest paper securities in the world. Real growth potential, however, is poor, because there is little change in the value of the principal. Liquidity is excellent. As an investment per se, these FAIL. As a "parking place," when considered as cash, CONSIDER.

MONEY MARKET FUNDS, GOVERNMENT ONLY Safety is very high, because of the underlying government securities, particularly if the fund only buys treasury bills. Real growth potential is poor due to very low interest rates. Liquidity is excellent, usually with check writing privileges. As an investment per se, FAIL. As a parking place for funds not invested, or as a cash reserve, CONSIDER.

TREASURY NOTES AND TREASURY BONDS These direct obligations of the federal government, with maturities of up to thirty years, are currently very safe. (This will change as federal budget deficits continue to worsen.) Real growth potential, because bond prices always fluctuate as interest rates change, particularly for the longest maturities, is excellent. Direct purchase involves small commissions, and this market is extremely liquid. For practiced investors, this investment passes our test. For small novice investors, because of the potential complexity in how to buy and sell, CONSIDER.

LOADED TREASURY BOND FUNDS Safety is similar to treasury bonds themselves. Real growth potential is much less because of sales and/or redemption fees. Physical liquidity is better than for individual issues, but psychological liquidity is less due to sales commissions. No-load funds are superior (see next item).

NO-LOAD TREASURY BOND FUNDS Safety and real growth potential are excellent. Liquidity is excellent, with no purchase or sales commission. PASS

GOVERNMENT AGENCY BONDS There are several government agencies. But the most common such securities are GNMAs and FNMAs (which are mortgage-backed securities). These are not direct obligations of the federal government and with real estate starting to suffer dramatically, we must rate these issues as only slightly above average for safety. Real growth potential is only average, because if interest rates rise these bonds fall in price, and if interest rates fall, people refinance home loans and return your money early. Liquidity is above average, but commissions can be a problem. FAIL

CORPORATE BONDS Safety is all over the board, depending on the company issuing the bond. Some are junk bonds already, and some are quite safe. Over the next four years, safety (and therefore prices) will fall dramatically for the majority of such bonds. Growth potential for long-term bonds is high, as prices move inversely to interest rates. For liquidity, commissions are higher than for treasuries, and the market for many issues is quite thin (not traded often). In summary, except for professional investors, this area will be a mine field over the next four years because of safety problems. FAIL

MUNICIPAL BONDS Safety is below average. This might surprise you, but the ability to pay interest and return principal is a direct function of a municipality's success in collecting taxes from constituents. This ability will be severely tested over the next four years, and many states and local governments are already in terrible shape. Real growth potential is possible because prices move inversely to interest rates. But the safety

❖ *Evaluation* ❖

consideration cannot be ignored, and prices will fall faster due to safety problems than they will rise from lower interest rates. Liquidity for numerous agencies can be a problem because of thin markets, and this is further complicated by significant commissions. FAIL

REAL ESTATE Safety is above average, because of the underlying asset. This assumes full insurance is always maintained. Real growth potential is above average, because one can buy on margin, with typical down payments of 10 to 20%, or even 0%. But this is only true for inflationary periods. Massive losses would result in a deflation. Liquidity is among the lowest of any investment. Commissions are very high, but more importantly, it can take many months to sell. FAIL

REAL ESTATE TRUST DEEDS Safety is much lower for trust deeds than for direct real estate investments. Particularly for second mortgages. Real growth potential is above average during inflationary periods. Liquidity is slightly below average due to commissions and the lack of a sophisticated market for individual securities. FAIL

REAL ESTATE INVESTMENT TRUSTS (REITs) Safety is above average, assuming astute selection of properties and region by the sponsor. Real growth potential is above average during inflationary periods, but poor during deflationary periods. Liquidity is above average for most issues, although commissions detract. CONSIDER

INDIVIDUAL STOCKS Safety is above average, as it is normally rare for an established company to declare bankruptcy. And in such a case, the price will drop dramatically and seasoned investors can sell before failure. Real growth potential is above average, as prices obviously move, both up and down. Liquidity is above average, except for the smallest of issues. Commissions prevent liquidity from being higher. CONSIDER

LOADED STOCK MUTUAL FUNDS Safety is slightly higher than for individual stocks, because of the diversification offered from a basket of many different equities. Real growth potential is slightly less. Liquidity is aggravated because of purchase and redemption fees that can be quite substantial. No-load funds are superior (see next item).

NO-LOAD STOCK MUTUAL FUNDS Safety is better than for individual stocks, due to diversification. Real growth potential is slightly less for the same reasons. Liquidity is excellent, because there are no purchase or sales commissions. PASS

GOLD Safety is ultimate, assuming safe storage. Real growth potential is excellent, particularly during inflationary periods and late in a deflation. Liquidity is below average, because of commissions and the need to physically transfer gold. FAIL

NO-LOAD GOLD MINING STOCK FUNDS Safety is above average, as for other stocks. Real growth potential is high when inflation is a problem, and when safety of other investments become suspect, particularly late in deflations. Liquidity is high because there are no commissions and due to the ease of buying and selling. PASS

SILVER AND OTHER PRECIOUS METALS Safety is above average, due to physical possession or safe storage. Real growth potential is above average, particularly during inflationary periods, but poor during deflations, because of a drop in demand. Liquidity is below average, for delivery and storage reasons as well as commissions. FAIL

COLLECTIBLES This includes rare coins (including most gold coins), stamps, art, diamonds, antiques, etc. Safety is above average, due to possession and insurance. Real growth potential is high during periods of inflation, particularly if one buys and holds for longer periods. Growth is poor during

❖ *Evaluation* ❖

deflations. Liquidity is poor because commissions can be very high and the difference between buy and sell price can exceed 30%. This market is also much smaller and thinner than others, further detracting from liquidity. FAIL

LIMITED PARTNERSHIPS Safety is a function of the type of investments purchased, the timeliness of such investments, and the degree of leveraging used (as opposed to cash purchases). Real growth potential is limited and subject to the decision of the general partner(s). Liquidity is extremely poor, because it is generally difficult to dispose of one's interest before a given date. FAIL

ANNUITIES Safety is slightly above average. These instruments do not have a record of major defaults over the past several years, but this situation could change dramatically over the next four years. Real growth potential is below average, and actual return is often less than projected, particularly in later years. Liquidity is below average due to high sales commissions, and redemption fees are generally large, particularly in the first few years. FAIL

LIFE INSURANCE/GICs There are a bewildering number of combined insurance/investment products and other securities offered by insurance companies. Guaranteed investment contracts are one example, but they are not guaranteed by the federal government as one might assume from the name. Universal life insurance is also well-known. Insurance itself should never be bought as an investment but for protection. There has not been a significant risk of insurance company defaults over the past several years, but again this situation could become problematic over the next four years, and most insurance companies are big buyers of junk bonds and real estate. Real growth potential is below average, primarily because of the introduction of a middleman (the insurance company) into the equation. Liquidity is below average because of sales commissions and typical redemption costs. FAIL

COMMODITY FUTURES Safety is generally above average, based on recent history. However, because of the heavy leveraging of debt, the potential for default is certainly present within this market. Real growth potential is enormous, as is the potential for loss. One will basically make or lose large amounts of money in short periods of time. Liquidity is complex. One can quickly process buys and sells, and commissions are low, but because of limit moves it might not be possible to enter or exit positions for several days in a row. Some markets can be thin, but this is most often reflected by price volatility unless a limit move is dictated. Only professional investors with substantial capital should consider these contracts. Even then, the vast majority of individuals lose money in this market. FAIL

OPTIONS These securities allow one to make money in rising or falling markets. Options are used in many types of markets, including individual stocks, stock market indices, commodity futures, and real estate. Safety has been acceptable, but again, the potential for defaults is certainly present because of the enormous price leveraging. Real growth potential is significant, as is the potential for loss. Liquidity is below average both because of significant commissions and the fact that most other markets are more liquid. Again, this market should not be considered except by the most sophisticated investor. FAIL

YOUR OWN BUSINESS Safety tends to be low, primarily due to the enormous failure rate (in excess of 90%) for new businesses. This rate will climb even higher for most new ventures over the next four years. Real growth potential, as a result, is low for the average new business. However, for businesses that survive, growth potential is theoretically unlimited. Liquidity is extremely poor, as it is difficult to locate buyers, and it can take months or years to find an interested buyer and obtain a reasonable sales price. FAIL

❖ Evaluation ❖

The following is a summary of the above, with each investment consideration rated from 0-10, with 10 being highest. Those rating the best for that type of investment (e.g., bond funds versus bonds themselves) and those considered the most interesting for an overall investment strategy are indicated with an asterisk.

SUMMARY-EVALUATION OF INVESTMENTS

	Safety	Real Growth Potential	Liquidity
Certificates of Deposit	5	3	3
Money Market Funds (Typical)	4	3	9
Savings Bonds	9	4	4
Treasury Bills	9	3	8
Money Mkt Funds, Gov't Only	9	3	10
Treasury Bonds	8	9	8
Loaded T-Bond Funds	8	7	8
*No-Load T-Bond Funds	8	9	9
Government Agency Bonds	6	5	6
Corporate Bonds	1-7	8	3-6
Municipal Bonds	4	6	6
Real Estate	8	8	1
Real Estate Trust Deeds	5	7	4
*Real Estate Investment Trusts	6	7	7
Individual Stocks	7	8	7
Loaded Stock Mutual Funds	8	7	6
*No-Load Stock Mutual Funds	8	7	9

Gold	10	8	4
*No-Load Gold Stock Funds	8	8	9
Silver/Other Precious Metals	7	8	4
Collectibles	7	8	2
Limited Partnerships	3-6	6	0
Annuities	6	4	4
Life Insurance (As investment)	6	4	4
Commodity Futures	6	10	7
Options	5	8	4
Your Own Business	3	?	1

Only four investments pass our investment screen. Remember, we used these investment criteria because of the volatile and dangerous financial and economic period we are now entering. We are demanding that our investments be above average in Safety, Real Growth Potential, and Liquidity or we simply "Just say no."

We have already discussed the enormous likelihood of deflation over the next four years. This means we will probably devote little, if any, funds to Real Estate Investment Trusts or No-Load Stock Mutual Funds for at least the first part of that period. But conditions can change, so we will leave all four on our list for now.

If deflation is in the cards, we might want to take advantage of making money in those markets that decline dramatically. There is one way to do this so that we are not exposed to unlimited risk. (Unlimited risk is defined as the possibility of losing more than the original investment.) Options provide this capability. Even though they didn't pass our investment screen, we don't want to miss an interesting opportunity for big investment gains. So let's add options back into our list of investments and take a closer look a bit later. If there is a way to compensate for some of the problems in this area, let's not throw it out just yet.

❖ *Evaluation* ❖

There is one final consideration. We have nothing on our list to accommodate cash positions. What do we do when preferred investments aren't timely? We must provide for this important need. If our qualifying investments are primarily available through mutual funds, it would be nice to choose something available at those financial institutions. We have two types of money market funds from which to choose. The obvious best choice is money market funds that only buy treasury bills. This will be a safe, secure parking place when we're not invested elsewhere. So let's keep this investment open for our use as well.

We have sorted through all the numerous investment possibilities. Some do not make sense in a simple but very effective investment strategy—during any economic period. Others provide all the means necessary to assemble a common-sense investment program. We are left with the following on our shopping list:

- No-Load Treasury Bond Funds
- No-Load Gold Mining Stock Funds
- No-Load Common Stock Funds
- Real Estate Investment Trusts
- Options
- Money Market Funds that only buy treasury bills

But we have done more than pick the most appropriate or interesting investments for the next four years. We have also massively simplified the investment process! As stated before, one of the biggest mistakes made by investors is they usually buy securities they don't fully understand. We have greatly narrowed our focus. When confronted by a salesman offering the greatest of new or old investment products, we can simply check our list and say, "No thanks, I'm not interested." In Chapter Six we will also take a close look at each of the above. Rather than knowing just enough about many investments to make ourselves dangerous, we will be able to understand six very well. Simplify. Simplify. And only then find out everything you can about the most appropriate.

NOTE: One particular investment did not qualify. But I want everyone to be aware of how it basically works. This is because it's closely related to one very familiar investment remaining on our list, which we'll talk about later. I'm talking about commodity futures. The easiest way to understand futures is to think of them as an agreement to buy or sell something, on a certain date in the future, but at today's price. This allows one to profit from higher or lower prices, with a high degree of leveraging.

Each futures contract is for a certain large quantity of a commodity, currency, or financial product. These agreements are usually bought and sold for a profit before that date in the future, simply to profit from price changes in the meantime. Let's provide an example, for only one side of the equation, to get an idea of how they work.

You think prices will rise for kryptonite. You're not interested in actually taking delivery of the metal, because you don't want any, but simply want to trade a contract for profits. You agree to buy one contract amount, in June of the following year, at today's price. Lets' say one contract of this hypothetical material is for 500 pounds of the stuff, and today's price is $200 a pound. So you agree to buy one contract's worth, next June, for $100,000 (500 x $200). You put $10,000 (10%) down as margin, owing the rest in good faith. Let's say the price goes up 10%. You don't care why, whether it be inflation, supply/demand, or speculation. You can sell your contract to someone else for $110,000 before the final settlement date, and pocket a 100% profit on your investment. When prices are volatile, this could happen in less than one week!

However, let's say prices fall by 10%, and that contract is only worth $90,000. Two important things happen. First, you've lost $10,000 on your investment so far, and it could fall

❖ *Evaluation* ❖

even lower. Secondly, your broker will call you and ask you to cough up another $10,000 in good faith money. This is termed a margin call. Would you be interested in futures contracts? Why not? Give this a little thought now, particularly as to how you would feel emotionally and financially about this type of investment, and we'll come back to this example later.

5

Better Choices

*Most of the change we think we see in life
Is truths being in and out of favor.*
—Robert Frost

LET'S BRIEFLY REVIEW how far we've come, before pursuing a very exciting exercise in our new investment strategy.

In the section on "denial" we saw the true facts of the current economic and financial health of our country. It is disastrous, and we were surprised how bad it was—even worse than in 1929.

In the chapter on "humility," we admitted we really didn't understand what was happening, and were perhaps a little angry that we hadn't been appropriately advised of the truth. We learned that our lack of true understanding was because of our listening to our basic belief system about money, which was learned at an early age. This was further confused by false sources of information who had vested interests (investments) in what we did with our money.

In the "hope" chapter, we set aside our current belief system and learned exactly how inflation and deflation work. We realized that these two economic developments are the driving forces behind higher or lower investment prices, and that how we invest is a function of which period we are experiencing.

Next we made the important decision that forces well beyond our control exercise great power over our personal economies and finances. Those deflation and recession cycles are powerful influences on investments, and have been in place for thousands of years. But even though we can't control these cycles, by understanding how they work we can make more timely and profitable investment decisions.

In the last chapter we evaluated each type of investment, first to determine which areas we should inspect more closely, and second to understand which investments make the most sense over the next four years. We also listed how we are currently investing our money, and determined our amount and type of debt. In addition, we closely detailed our income and exactly how we spent our money. Not for judgment, but for better understanding.

Choices

It's now time to admit that our savings or investment techniques can be greatly improved. We don't yet have enough information to make changes in our capital investments for growth (the securities we buy), but it's time to plan changes and create opportunities within our personal investments involving consumption.

Stocks, bonds, and gold are investments. So are beer, cigarettes, clothing, and virtually anything else. By carefully choosing our consumption investments we can make more funds available for growth investments, speeding our financial serenity—without detracting from our happiness or a desirable lifestyle.

In the last chapter we listed our expenses, and gave some thought as to our motivation for each. Investments involve expectations, and we never do anything without a purpose. What are the possible purposes? Some make sense, and we decided that others just might not. Neither does the following exercise involve judgment. Only choices.

As soon as people fully realize that every $1 saved can be

❖ *Better Choices* ❖

turned into $20-30 in purchasing power by 1998, their interest in saving seems to increase for some reason. But I do not want you to become a money-grubbing miser, and create a new investment in greed. Our choices must augment our enjoyment of life and balance today's pleasures with tomorrow's dreams.

You will need to refer back to your analysis on spending from the last chapter. Also get your notes together on your possible motivation for those expenses. It's time to do some brainstorming and create a new budget.

As a family, tackle each expense item and develop a target budget. Be creative in carving savings out of old expense patterns, satisfying emotional needs less expensively, and using innovative ways to enjoy life even more. This is done with simple choices. And any expense item provides the opportunity to:

- Increase savings for investment opportunities
- Buy fewer but more satisfying similar items
- Spend additional amounts in a more important area

We must introduce another ground rule, however. Those potential savings from expenses that are uniquely personal must not be planned by the group, but offered by the individual himself without any pressure from others in the family.

When each person is committed to the process, the family will benefit dramatically. This is generally the case. The biggest problem, however, is when one family member accounts for a lopsided percentage of miscellaneous expenses and is also uncooperative. If your family is creative, you might work out a unique and harmonious way of handling this. If not, the most loving solution is for others to simply do their own best, and accept one family member's current difficulty in cutting expenses.

I guarantee you that a surprising amount of potential savings lies in such personal areas. It's a virtual gold mine. Impulsive cash outlays and credit card purchases really add up. But regardless of how successful your family is at tapping this source, don't forget one thing. Always allow each family member a certain amount of cash, or mad money, each month, regardless of how much that amount might be. This provides a certain degree of freedom for each, and helps avoid self-imposed guilt for those impulsive purchases that will inevitably occur.

Be aggressive and creative. But don't plan complex ways to save small amounts for investment. We're trying to enhance our current and future lives, not complicate them. It is for this reason that I never recommend families go nuts on coupon clipping, unless they already have a comfortable habit of doing so. On the other hand, if you have younger children they might be willing to do the job if there's also enough motivation. If they received half the savings there could be a nice sense of cooperation, and a few extra dollars a week for them might be encouraging and fun. The following work sheet will be helpful.

TARGET BUDGET

HOUSING	Mortgage/Rent	$_____
	Lawn/Garden	_____
	House Repairs	_____
	Real Estate Tax	_____
HOUSEHOLD	New Furniture/Appliances	_____
	Appliance Repairs	_____
	Purchase Misc. Items	_____
UTILITIES	Electricity	_____
	Oil/Gas	_____
	Telephone	_____

❖ *Better Choices* ❖

FOOD/MISC PERSONAL _____

CLOTHING   Him _____
                     Her _____

_____   _____
_____   _____
_____   _____

CASH ALLOWANCES/MISC PERSONAL
                 Him _____
                 Her _____

_____   _____
_____   _____
_____   _____

AUTOMOBILE   Loan Payments _____
                    Gas/Oil _____
                    Repairs/Tires _____
                    Tax/License _____

MEDICAL/DRUGS _____

INSURANCE   Auto _____
                 Life _____
                 Household _____
                 Medical _____
                 Disability _____

CHARITY/CHURCH _____

CHRISTMAS/OTHER GIFTS _____

MISC GIFTS _____

ENTERTAIN/RECREATION/
   MEALS OUT _____

❖ Debt-Free In Four Years ❖

VACATIONS   _____

CLUBS/ORGANIZATIONS   _____

COLLEGE   _____

SELF-EDUCATION/GROWTH   _____

CHILD SUPPORT   _____

SPOUSAL SUPPORT   _____

ACCOUNTANT/TAX PREP   _____

OTHER PROFESSIONAL FEES   _____

CREDIT CARDS,
MONTHLY PAYMENTS   _____

OTHER LOAN REPAYMENTS   _____

OTHER   _____   _____

                _____   _____

                _____   _____

SAVINGS   _____   _____

                            MONTHLY TOTAL $_____

  Notice that this format is slightly different from our expense sheet, because we now reintroduce repayment of old loans and credit card balances. We also add savings.
  It's suggested you first conduct your expense review to find savings without the tips which follow at the end of this

❖ *Better Choices* ❖

chapter. It will be more fun to brainstorm without guidelines, because it keeps the mind more open for unique ideas that are truly yours. When you've exhausted all your personal ideas, only then resort to that list for additional opportunities.

By keeping track of purchases you decide against making, and the resulting savings, you will be amazed at how much you can set aside. It's not unusual for families to find an additional $1000 to $2500 a year. And if we can invest this new Found Money aggressively, each $1000 found today can mean $20,000-30,000 in purchasing power in only four years.

One final, but extremely important point: Plan a receptacle—a separate account or piggy bank—to actually receive the family's new Found Money until it's physically invested. If this is not done, this money too will be destined to the same fate money usually is. It will simply be...spent.

It's a good idea to also discuss, and then separately list, larger planned purchases. This will help you set money aside so funds are available exactly when needed. It also helps avoid confusing your monthly budget. Depending on the category totals, you then divide by twelve, and enter above. You might want to do the same for quarterly, semi-annual, or other non-monthly expenses, for the same reasons.

There's a related, extremely effective, variation of this technique. List non-monthly payments and planned purchases on the following sheet, in the month they will be incurred. Calculate a Base Total of regular monthly budget expenses that does not include these items. Add the two together, and you achieve a quite accurate advance total of expenses for each month. Add an appropriate reserve and you have the total you will require in your checking account going into that month. Anything extra can then be "swept" into your investments with only one check every month. This is a very professional approach and allows you to really work your money hard. Funds aren't sitting in a checking account collecting little, if any, interest. And they're still accessible with a check on that money fund, if really needed.

EXPENSES/PLANNED PURCHASES BY MONTH

NON-MONTHLY ITEM	AMOUNT	BASE AMOUNT	MO. TOTAL

JAN
_____ _____
_____ _____ _____ _____
_____ _____

FEB
_____ _____
_____ _____ _____ _____
_____ _____

MAR
_____ _____
_____ _____ _____ _____
_____ _____

APR
_____ _____
_____ _____ _____ _____
_____ _____

❖ *Better Choices* ❖

MAY

JUN

JLY

AUG

SEP

OCT

NOV

DEC

Found Money Tips

The following are additional ideas to generate more Found Money. Some you will have already identified. And your family has probably even come up with ideas not discussed:

When buying another car, find a good three-year old. Hertz has researched the subject and found a three-year old is the lowest in total owning and operating costs. Much of the fastest depreciation on resale value is already gone from the price, major components are still in good shape, and those small annoying repairs won't be encountered for years to come. *Consumer Reports Buying Guide* can help choose the most trouble-free. Take a candidate to a good mechanic and have him check it out. He can also provide input on his experience with that model and year. You can even make some modifications, like installing a new stereo, etc., and still save $1500 a

❖ Better Choices ❖

year with this idea alone, simply by not buying new cars.

At least for the next four years, replace your whole life insurance with term insurance. You might even have cash value in a current policy, that you can put to work. This is often the only source of capital available to many people.

Stop over-withholding on income taxes. If you get money back, you're over-withholding. I know Uncle Sam sorely needs the money, but why lend it to him for fifteen months? Without interest! This is done by increasing the number of exemptions filed with your employer. Even if you end up with more than the total actual number. After all, that's only a guideline to estimate withholding. Most people are afraid of penalties. The tax code currently states you will not be penalized if you 1) Withhold the same as your actual taxes from the year prior, or 2) Withhold 90% of your eventual taxes due for the tax year in question, whichever is less. Check with your accountant before doing this, because laws constantly change. It's suggested you place the extra cash flow in a safe money market fund—a separate account if possible—to keep it in reserve for writing a check at tax time for amount due. Collect interest on your own money for a change.

Another thing to check with your accountant is how you can give money to your children, and make the same investments you normally would. The family's Found Money is the difference in taxes between your rate and the children's lower tax rates.

Quit buying commissioned securities. Any commissions you would have paid are Found Money.

Many people automatically spend more money if they have a credit card. If you are disciplined and can easily resist the temptation, another Found Money approach is possible. Many credit cards don't charge any interest if the balance is fully paid every month. By buying as much as possible with such cards, and paying the full balance every month, you get up to thirty days additional cash flow. This is like an interest-free loan. Just make sure you don't buy more expensive items only because the more appropriate store doesn't accept your card.

❖ *Debt-Free In Four Years* ❖

By paying cash with certain people for various things, you can negotiate lower prices. This doesn't work with most stores. But particularly when dealing with individuals, you'll be surprised how much less the person will take when they see the hard, cold cash.

Use checking accounts that pay some kind of interest. This might take a few phone calls, but such financial institutions are out there. Just don't maintain balances higher than needed simply to meet a minimum for earning interest. Another approach is to use the base account of your investment program, your money market account, for larger payments every month. With check minimums of only $100 in most cases, your money will be earning a nice interest rate until the day your check on the account clears. This is preferable to keeping the money in a checking account that often doesn't pay any interest at all. This obviously doesn't work for payments of less than $100.

Consider consolidating your debt, such as the amounts on all your credit cards, etc. If you can arrange a lower monthly payment and/or lower interest rate, then better cash flow and lower interest expense can result. But make sure you're totally informed of loan generation fees, or other costs, before taking out the consolidation loan. Are there any costs for paying off the new loan early? It's not hard to beat typical interest rates of 18% or more on credit cards. New cards also often have lower interest rates. If you are eligible, roll higher card balances into a new, lower rate arrangement.

Consider share rentals, particularly if you're single. Many people have too much house for their income. By renting out a room and sharing certain other parts of the house, additional income can be gained. These situations most often result from the high divorce rate. One of the parties ends up with the house but doesn't want to sell it. Share rentals are the resulting opportunities. More people are also renting large apartments together. This is not just an idea for young people. Everyone benefits from lower outlays.

Most people have a great amount of money in the garage,

❖ *Better Choices* ❖

in tools they rarely use and tons of miscellaneous other items. Have a garage sale and you will simplify your life greatly and obtain increased investment funds. When you periodically require a special tool, the local rental house should have it. You will also save a lot of time by having someone else complete certain repairs. Are your time and freedom important to you?

Here are several other miscellaneous ideas people are using:

- Buying quality used instead of new
- Planning and discussing certain expenses, instead of impulsively buying
- Smart thermostat (programmable)
- Ceiling fan...to cut heating/air conditioning costs
- More letters; fewer long distance phone calls
- Generic cigarettes, bought by the carton, not by the pack
- Buy more food at warehouse food stores
- Different, less expensive snacks, like fruit
- Drinks after work at home instead of at a lounge, for huge cost savings
- Ride sharing
- Fewer lunches out; more often take quality lunches
- Fewer, better-quality clothes
- Get quotes on insurance for equal quality and less cost; increase deductibles?
- Generic drugs
- More personal and unique, perhaps handcrafted gifts; fewer typical purchased items
- Different, creative, but more enjoyable recreation activities
- Ask handy friends for help with

repairs...in exchange for a favor?
- More home entertainment; less out
- Use accountant for taxes; pay with more deductions
- Plan purchases; pay cash to reduce credit card interest

So happy hunting! And don't forget to consider emotional ties to old spending patterns. As you identify and deal with them, the personal and financial rewards are enormous during a period of unprecedented change.

6

Focus and Courage

Courage leads starward, fear toward death.
—Seneca

IN CHAPTER FOUR we evaluated all types of investments for their appropriateness. We want to be particularly careful over the next four years. This is why we demand above-average Safety, above-average Real Growth Potential, *and* above-average Liquidity.

Certain investments qualified; others did not. Another reason for that review was to simplify our investment approach. I've noticed over the years that investors usually place their money in investments and with financial institutions without really understanding what they're doing. One reason for this problem is there are simply too many investment vehicles available today. It's virtually impossible to become experts in them all. So when a salesman bears down on us we often capitulate if the pitch sounds good, and we buy.

Most people have some people pleasing patterns and often will not ask the hard and fast questions necessary to determine the facts. Being nice can be an attractive quality, but not when it means doing something you don't understand. The "all knowing" individual also encounters problems. When you're trying to play the "I know" and "macho" role the same mistakes can be made, simply because one doesn't want others to think he might not be knowledgeable. These reasons not only help explain why bad investments are chosen, but from whom we buy them. We then feel cheated when the investment's value heads south, the financial institution fails, or the guy disappears with our money.

When we don't understand, our decision-making process can be severely hampered. Maybe we don't trust anyone. One solution to this faith problem is to put our money only with what we *think* are the safest institutions. Millions of people are barely covering inflation and taxes in such investments. And how truly safe are they? How do they really invest that money? Our lack of understanding prevents us from even asking the appropriate questions. I guarantee that what appears to be safe today will be dramatically different, perhaps overnight, during the next four years.

Another solution to the trust problem is spreading our investments all over the place to avoid single disasters. This action first greatly complicates our life because they're so difficult to keep track of. And even if we've avoided the possibility of major disasters, we're still subject to a series of minor explosions with the same end result. One old standard phrase is, "Don't put all your eggs in one basket." Others say, "First understand exactly what you're doing. Then put all your eggs in one basket, and make damn sure nobody upsets it."

Some people claim they're diversifying when they're not. One investor might feel he's diversified by buying several different stocks. Another might think he's doing the job by buying CDs from several different financial institutions. Neither understands the term; and the one is subject to an overall decline in the stock market and the other is vulnerable to broad problems within the banking system. True diversification means buying different types of investments. Now that you know how different investments fluctuate in price over certain periods, and given the most probable developments over the next four years, diversification in the following makes the most sense: A treasury bond fund, a gold mining stock fund, and a government-only money market fund.

❖ *Focus and Courage* ❖

Diversification can be appropriate, and concentration of investments can make sense. But understanding always makes sense. By limiting our investments to the most sensible, we can now look into each remaining area carefully, and understand exactly how it works. This strengthens our courage to make the most appropriate decisions.

Four investments rated the highest from our investment test. We then added two others to round out a complete investment strategy, which gives us the means of taking advantage of all the most likely changes over the next four years.

We can now fully concentrate our attention in six areas:

- No-Load Common Stock Mutual Funds
- No-Load Treasury Bond Funds
- No-Load Gold Mining Stock Funds
- Real Estate Investment Trusts
- Options
- Money Market Funds that hold treasury bills

To completely understand each, it's necessary to first know how stocks, bonds, gold, real estate, options, and money market funds work as investments.

Common Stocks

When you buy a stock, you become part owner of the company. The owner of any company has the right to help determine the management, vote on major company decisions, share in the profits, and sell his interest to another.

When the company earns a profit, the Board of Directors decides to do one of three things with those proceeds. They can decide to make investments with those funds. More typically, they either use the money to further improve the firm in various ways (for growth), or to distribute it among the owners (shareholders) as a dividend.

Young companies, or rapidly-growing companies, generally use a large percentage of profits to expand the company.

Growth companies, as they're called, might not appear to be good investments because the shareholder doesn't receive as much in dividends, if he receives anything at all. However, if the company is truly growing and the money is used appropriately, the company will benefit in the future. The result should be higher stock prices later instead of dividends today.

One major mistake many novice investors make is to purchase stocks simply because they pay high dividends. Such stocks will not tend to move as much in price as those paying lower dividends. But this does not mean they're good investments, because the share price can drop dramatically. In fact, dividends will be even less important over the next four years than they have been previously. Do you think that even the investor collecting 10% dividends in October, 1987, was worried about dividends? No, he was worried about the value of his investment. In only one day, such investors lost twice the amount in share value than they would have received in two year's worth of dividends. This trend will likely continue in the future, even if at a less dramatic pace.

Another major investment problem is "getting married" to your stock. This is often the case when you work for that company, or if that stock has done very well for you in the past. Perhaps you've done your research well and have uncovered an excellent company. Should you buy it? The best stock in the world will decline sharply in price if the economy and the rest of the stock market decline. "When the cops raid the house of ill repute, they take the good girls with the bad."

Stock prices fluctuate due to three major reasons:

- The company's changing fortunes
- Investor psychology (greed, panic, etc...)
- Economic change

Let's discuss each. We've already talked about two major stock investment errors, but not the most important one. The greatest cause of stock investment losses involves "news." Someone, even a broker, tells you of some exciting develop-

❖ *Focus and Courage* ❖

ment about a stock. Some future change or company plan is said to be good for the stock and the price should rise. The information makes sense, and even turns out to be true. Do you buy? No.

This is because financial institutions and professional investors knew that same information long before you did, have already bought, and the price already reflects that news. In other words, smart money and big money, which truly drive market prices, have already acted. It's true that several people will hear that news item after you do, and also buy. But their buying has to exceed the selling by profit-takers who purchased early.

The appropriateness of any investment is determined by the number of buyers and sellers who follow your purchase decision. This means you *must* see something attractive about a stock or any other investment that most other people haven't yet recognized. It's this final realization that forms the bandwagon that drives prices higher. What everyone knows in investing isn't worth knowing.

This is why prices of stocks reflect *future* anticipated events, *not today's news*. The stock market serves as a barometer, not a thermometer, of the economy.

One very common misconception about the stock market involves something called a stock split. A company decides that if the price of its shares were lower, more people might be interested in buying their stock. In such a case they adjust the price downwards and also adjust the number of shares outstanding to compensate for this. If you had 100 shares at $50 dollars each, in a 2 for 1 split you find yourself holding 200 shares at $25 each. Big deal; both before and after you have $5000 of stock. But because the public thinks this is a great thing, professionals often take advantage of this false belief. What often happens is professionals buy on the announcement of a split and sell when it becomes effective. So much for that windfall.

Although it's not important to our strategy, you should be familiar with one other stock term called a short sale. This is a way to make money when the stock market declines. The procedure is to find a stock you think will fall in price. Let's say the price is $80 a share. You borrow someone else's shares from your broker and sell them. If the stock price declines as expected, you then buy them back at a lower price, say $60 a share, making $20 a share. If the price rises, however, you might have to buy them back at a much higher price. Potential loss is theoretically unlimited. When you buy stocks outright, maximum loss is what you paid. Many people who don't understand the stock market feel it's a big gamble. But those same people often turn around and start their own businesses. What's the difference? For one thing, the odds are at least 90% that a new business will fail. Listed stocks, on the other hand, have been in existence for years, probably decades. They've established the fact they can make money and survive. This doesn't mean stocks don't default by declaring bankruptcy, and many will do just that over the next four years. But the odds of losing money in the stock market are less than when starting your own business.

If your business is one of the few that become highly successful, you will eventually want to do many things that stocks on listed exchanges do. You can borrow money by issuing debt securities (bonds), and might even want to sell part of your interest with stock sales. You might even decide to take your company public and become one of the "bad guys." The stock and bond markets are therefore important to the way our country operates.

So should you buy stocks? There are periods when they are great investments. There are also periods when they must be totally avoided. Stocks do, however, play an important role in most investment strategies. Investors should instead determine the best way to invest in the stock market.

We've already discussed some serious complications to making money in this market. Nevertheless, many average investors still try to beat the professionals by buying individual stocks. In order to consistently make money buying indi-

❖ *Focus and Courage* ❖

vidual stocks you must do several things.

At a minimum, your research must anticipate developments concerning a stock—before that information becomes common knowledge.

You might think your broker can provide this information. Stop and think for a moment, and even ask your broker, "Where did this information come from?" Nine times out of ten it came from the brokerage company's main research group. Where did the research group obtain the information? Most likely from analysts who closely watch all major companies. The next question is, "What makes you think you're among the first people receiving this information?" Does it stand to reason that major institutions would receive the news before you were called?

You must also be smarter and faster than the insiders. These are people privy to major developments before anyone else. They are the top management, and in the case of "deals" and takeovers, the investment bankers, lawyers, and accountants are putting the deal together and all their friends. Good luck.

You also have to compete with professional investors who spend ten hours a day closely watching the markets. What we're explaining is that the small investor is generally "the last to know." Any information you use to buy stocks still has to be gained by looking at the market in a unique way, and thereby seeing something others do not. I would only use information provided by brokers who do their own research and aren't simply passing down some news from headquarters. There are a few such rare animals out there, but one still should never use such information to buy unless he were confident that most other investors haven't yet anticipated the development.

It is for all these reasons I seldom suggest that an investor buy individual stocks. Even the most intelligent of business owners are not impervious to the land mines listed above. I suggest no-load mutual funds, which we will discuss later.

Treasury Bonds

Treasury bonds are direct obligations of the federal government. When you buy a treasury bond, you are lending money to our government. There are five terms you should understand about bonds:

- Par Value
- Coupon Rate
- Maturity Date
- Call Date
- Yield

The par value is the amount that will be returned at maturity. If you buy a newly-issued bond, this is also the price you pay, excluding any commissions.

The coupon rate is the percent interest the bond pays, expressed as a percentage of par value.

The maturity date is when the final owner receives repayment of par value, if the bond issuer doesn't default. We say final owner because most bonds are bought and sold several times before maturity.

Call date. Some bonds can be retired or called, which means that the par value is repaid before maturity. This allows the issuer to, in effect, refinance at a lower interest rate.

Yield is the interest you receive as a percentage of your investment. A bond's price changes, so dividing coupon rate by your cost determines yield. (Yield to maturity is more complex and won't be discussed in this synopsis.) The following explains how to read a typical newspaper price statement for a bond, and is a good review of these definitions.

10 3/8 Nov 04-09   113:02   113:08   +19   8.83

10 3/8 is the coupon rate. This bond pays $10.38 interest a year (usually in two semi-annual payments) for each $100 of par value.

❖ *Focus and Courage* ❖

Nov 04-09 means the bond matures in November 2009, but can be called on or after the year 2004. If interest rates drop far enough by that time, it might behoove the issuer to pay off the bond (at par) and reissue new bonds at lower rates.

113:02 is the bid price at which potential buyers are offering to buy the bond.

113:08 is the asked price at which holders are offering to sell their bond. Transactions will occur between these two prices.

+19 is the price change of the bond that day.

8.83 is the yield, which is the yearly interest percentage you would receive on your investment if you purchased the bond at that day's price. Except for yield and coupon rate, the numbers following the decimal point are 1/32s. For example, the bid price, asked price, and price change are really 113 2/32, 113 8/32, and 19/32 respectively. This might sound crazy, but it's simply convention for the bond market.

Bonds used to be called the investment of "widows and orphans." This description might have been appropriate thirty years ago when interest rates changed very little. With the advent of inflation, however, interest rates undergo massive change. As a result, long-term bonds in particular can experience price changes as great as those of stocks. We will see how prices change in a moment.

One of the greatest misconceptions about bonds is that they have to be held until maturity. You do not have to hold a bond to maturity. When I suggest a thirty-year bond, the usual response is "I don't want to tie up my money for that long." In fact, most investors don't hold a bond until maturity. And treasury bonds, in particular, are even more liquid (actively traded) investments than stocks.

This means there must be a way to price bonds when they are bought and sold before maturity. The market is extremely efficient in doing so. Market price changes for bonds are a function of changing interest rates, and vice versa. If you're certain you understand this process, please skip the next few paragraphs. If not, please continue.

❖ *Debt-Free In Four Years* ❖

Most people become very confused about bond prices and interest rates. In seminars I arrived at an analogy that greatly simplifies the explanation. Bonds are like dairy cows. Here are the rules for our cattle market example:

- New dairy cows are always sold at $100 (just like new bonds are always sold at $100 par).
- You can buy/sell used cows at any time, at the price the market will bear.
- You can turn in your used cows at some specific time in the future (if alive) for $100.

Let's say you bought a new cow in 1978 for 100. Its yield was eight quarts a day. But by 1981 new cows were yielding 16 quarts a day. What would have happened to the price of your 1978 model used cow? If new cows always sell for 100, it would have taken two of yours to yield the same milk. So the price of your critter would have fallen to about 50, particularly if it were several years before you could turn it back in. The price was marked down to produce the same yield (8/50 = 16%) as a new cow. This is exactly what happens to bond prices. If interest rates go up after you buy, the price of your bond will decline to a price that reflects the same percentage yield as new issues. In fact, during the same period as our example bond prices fell dramatically, as interest rates soared.

If you buy a new bovine that yields 8 quarts (8%), and later the new models only yield 4 (4%), the market price of your cow will roughly double (8/200 = 4%). By the same token, if you buy a long-term bond and interest rates then fall, the price of your bond will naturally rise.

So there are two very important things potential bond buyers must never forget. First, bond prices move *inversely* to interest rates. When interest rates go down, bond prices rise. When rates rise, bond prices fall. Second, always avoid bonds

❖ *Focus and Courage* ❖

when interest rates might rise. And buy bonds for price appreciation, which can be dramatic, when interest rates are destined to fall.

It should be noted that long-term bonds (with several years to maturity) move the most in price with changing interest rates. On the other hand, short-term bonds move less in price as rates change. The reason for this is short-term bonds are close to redemption at full par value. So they won't be priced to a significant discount (price decline) or rise to much of a premium (above par value). If you are very conservative, you will want to concentrate on short maturities. If you want the greatest opportunity for capital gains, use the longest maturities.

Two real examples will illustrate. Interest rates were high in 1981, and moved lower into 1983. On September 25, 1981, a four-year treasury bond was quoted at a price of 81. A twenty-six year treasury bond was quoted at 70. Interest rates then fell, and bond prices increased. On March 3, 1983, the same short-term bond was quoted at 98 and the long-term bond at 99. The short-term bond increased in price 21%, and the long-term bond jumped 42% in price! Of course interest was also received on these securities during the period they were held. Bonds are no longer dull, boring investments by any stretch of the imagination.

How is the interest rate determined on newly-issued bonds? You might even have thought they were fixed on a take-it-or-leave-it basis. This is untrue. If rates are fixed too low, all the bonds simply won't be sold. In fact, new bonds take their cue from the secondary market. What is considered a fair interest rate for "used bonds" determines interest rates for new bonds of similar maturity length. If a particularly large bond offering is made, issuers still might incorrectly estimate the interest rate necessary to sell such bonds. In such a case, buyers might even force a change in rates, and the bonds end up being sold at a small discount, or even a premium.

If bond prices are a function of interest rates, it's important to know what affects rates. Four major factors affect interest rates at any point in time. These are:

- Supply/demand for bonds, and profit   2%
- Risk   0%
- Taxability   2%
- Inflation   3%

                                                            ———
                                                            7%

The above numbers are approximate for today's long-term treasury bonds. Let's discuss each factor.

If supply is low (few new issues, or people don't want to sell), or demand is high (many people wanting to buy), a bond will tend to rise in price, driving down interest rates. It's simply not necessary for a bond to pay as high an interest rate to attract buyers. On the other hand, a high supply or low demand will force interest rates higher to attract more buyers. There must also be some profit for the person lending the money.

Risk is very important. If risk is high, interest rates will be much higher to compensate for the danger of default. The safest bonds will yield the lowest interest rates. Treasury bonds are currently risk-free, but this will change.

If a bond is tax-free, interest will be lower. If taxable, the yield will be higher.

Inflation is the most volatile component of interest rates, and reflects the decline in purchasing power of returned principal. If inflation is at 3%, the value of your principal will fall in purchasing power by 3% over the next year. If you were to lend someone money for one year and inflation is 3%, you will demand at least 3% interest rates for this factor alone, even before considering the other three factors.

We add these factors to yield an approximate total interest rate at any point in time. It might surprise you that in terms of interest rates alone, if you subtract the yearly loss from inflation and adjust for taxes, even today the real gain is only in the range of 2%.

Deflation is the scenario of highest probability over the next four years. So let's compare total interest rates now compared to a period of deflation—when the value of the dollar increases and the Consumer Price Index is negative.

	1995	Deflation
- Supply/demand/profit	2%	2%
- Risk	0%	0%
- Taxability	2%	2%
- Inflation	3%	-2%
	7%	2%

It might sound preposterous to consider 2% interest rates. But over long periods of time 2% interest rates are not unusual. The insanity of rates over the last 30 years has become fact, has become normal! Simply because of inflation.

With a clear understanding of how bonds work, one can even entertain the possibility of negative interest rates. Why would you lend your money to someone at negative interest? There are two reasons. First, in a deflation, the value of your principal in purchasing power will be greater when returned than when lent. But more importantly, with the prices of virtually every other investment plummeting in value, if you could be absolutely sure the issuer would return your money you might do so for safety purposes. Swiss banks, which are considered extremely safe, sometimes pay negative interest on money. This factor will become more obvious as deflation unfolds.

I want to specifically address those people who believe hyperinflation (massively higher inflation rates) is a serious current danger. This can occur in any country, but greatly depends on the location of debt. Today, all three American entities are massively in debt: The government, companies, and individuals. A huge and very sophisticated bond market that fully understands the effect of inflation on interest rates will not allow hyperinflation. If inflation even rose to only 10% again, the bond market would collapse, and bonds would plunge in price. This would force interest rates up hard. It would take only about six months of interest rates above 14% for the economy to be forced into a hard downward tailspin...that would cause interest rates to eventually decline because of falling inflation.

Investors have three reasons for buying treasury bonds:

- Interest Income
- Appreciation (buy low, sell high)
- Protection Against Deflation

Over the next four years, interest income will be a less-important factor. With the value of your principal, as reflected by the bond price, jumping around all over the place, bond prices will be the most important. As in October, 1987, do you think investors were concerned about income (dividends) as the value of their stocks plummeted by 22% in only one day?

Appreciation, the ability to buy a volatile investment at a low price (higher interest rates) and to sell at higher prices when interest rates plummet, will be a key reason for bond investment.

Protection against deflation! We finally have a way to invest during a period of falling prices and wages. Remember we're only talking about treasury bonds—direct obligations of the federal government. There will be massive defaults in virtually all other bond areas. As inflation rates drop, and turn negative, interest rates will plummet and bond prices will soar. If, as in the above example, rates drop from 7% to 2%, we're looking at a probable three-fold increase in the prices of long-term treasury bonds. (This assumes the federal government does not approach bankruptcy. This remains to be seen.)

Aggressive investors in particular will also be interested in

❖ *Focus and Courage* ❖

treasury bonds that offer even more price leverage than the longest treasuries. These are called zero coupon bonds. Here is how they work.

Everyone is familiar with savings bonds. They don't pay interest per se, but are bought at a discount. You might pay $17.50 for the bond, which increases in price every year until it matures at $25. These are a form of zero coupon bonds. Treasury bills are also zeros. If interest rates are about 10% you would pay about $9,090 for a one year bill. At the end of one year you receive $10,000. Again, you don't receive interest per se, but the price is discounted at purchase and "interest" is the difference between price paid and what you would receive at maturity. These are also a form of zero bonds.

What would you pay for a zero coupon treasury bond that pays you $100 in 30 years, if interest rates were 13% today? Remember, you receive no interest in the interim, but this is reflected in price increases until maturity. You might have to play with your calculator a bit, but a fair price would be about $2.56. (Multiply 1.13 times 2.56, thirty times, and you get 100.) If interest rates fell to 2% by 1998 in a deflation, the price of your bond would rise to $60. Excluding commissions, the value of your investment would rise twenty-fold. If interest rates went from 7% to 2%, the increase would be 4.6 times. And remember, in only a 3-to-1 deflation, your purchasing power for the latter would be increased 14 times.

This example assumed a thirty-year bond. But again, zeros of shorter maturity will be less volatile in price, and also provide less appreciation potential.

This method of investing in treasury bonds is very interesting, and gives you more leverage than physical treasurys. But as you can sense, the price of a long-term zero coupon bond bounces around like popcorn. If you buy before a period of rising interest rates, the value of your zero bonds will get hit hard. But if we can develop a system to buy and sell at the right time, the rewards can be phenomenal.

This is one way to double investment values over the next

four years. If really aggressive, we can use the longest maturities for gains that exceed a four-fold price increase. In only a 3-to-1 deflation, purchasing power increases 6 and 14 times respectively.

Gold Mining Stocks

These are companies just like any other, except for what they do. They physically mine the gold that is then sold at market price. And we're not talking about fledgling mines that have yet to produce. The latter constitute the penny stock arena, when above-ground promises and excitement often exceed the amount of gold below-ground.

We are instead focusing on the listed stocks of companies that have been mining gold for many years, usually several decades. They are both producing and also have proven reserves of gold to be mined in the future.

We cannot discuss mining stocks, however, without considering how the price of their product changes.

Most people fall into one of three categories in their opinion of gold. They love it, hate it, or don't understand it. Gold has been described both as a "barbarous relic" and the backbone of worldwide finance. In reality, there are certain periods when it plays an important role, and other times when it is relatively unimportant. Gold is not very useful when a nation's currency is stable and predictable. But it plays a crucial role when other forms of money are suspect, when inflation is present, or when the economic situation is volatile. Unfortunately, we have been experiencing the latter conditions on a worldwide scale for the last thirty years.

One important question is "what is money?" A piece of paper printed by a government, a computer number on a bank statement, or a questionable promise? Aristotle is credited with most of the following definitions of the ideal currency:

- Rare, and cannot be created by a government
- Durable

❖ Focus and Courage ❖

- Of consistent quality and purity is easily measured
- Easily divisible and portable
- Intrinsic value (certain practical uses)

Gold obviously fits this description better than anything else in the world, which is why it has been used as a currency for thousands of years. But in a highly technological world like today, the use of actual gold is impractical. So countries stored gold and issued gold certificates, that represented a claim on the stored metal. Unfortunately, no government in history has ever resisted the temptation to abuse a currency every few decades by printing more money than is backed by the precious metal. In the free market, the value of the currency then falls and purchases less. But rather than indexes showing the drop in currency value, prices appear to rise, and this is called "inflation."

This has occurred hundreds of times, and in virtually every country in the world. On several occasions inflation progressed to such levels that the currency became worthless. The U.S. has a history of seriously abusing its currency every 50-100 years. In the 1920s much money was printed, but that fact went largely unnoticed because the economy was growing so fast. In the 1860s inflation averaged more than 25% a year over a three year period. Between 1776 and 1780, inflation averaged more than 200% a year before the Continental Dollar became worthless.

Our recent problems started in the 1950s. The U.S. dollar was supposedly backed by gold, but Washington continued to print dollars. However, only foreign holders could exchange their dollars for gold. By 1960, dollars held overseas (called Eurodollars) had grown to equal our total gold holdings, when valued at the "official" price of $35/ounce. By 1971 Nixon was forced to stop allowing foreigners to exchange their dollars for our gold.

The U.S. continued to print money and the situation deteriorated further. By 1974 it would have been necessary for gold reserves to be worth $280 an ounce just to back all the dollars located outside the U.S. (not counting the money supply within the country).

The situation was clearly out of hand, and it was no longer possible to pretend the dollar was even partially backed by gold. No longer a "monetary metal," gold could again be legally owned by U.S. citizens. Today, *no currency in the world is backed by gold.*

Various factors influence the price. (In reality, we should turn this statement around and ask what affects the value of a paper or computer dollar in terms of ounces of gold per dollar, but this might be confusing to some.)

Supply versus demand is one factor. But new production of gold each year adds only about 2% to the above-ground supply. Although gold is used in certain applications, demand is primarily a function of how many people are seeking a safe haven in times of economic turmoil.

Political developments also play a role. But again, this is more a function of how changes might affect monetary stability. Military influences can be important, but are generally short-lived.

The most important factor is economic. When inflation exists, gold rises in value to reflect the less-valuable dollar in which it is priced. It depreciates during recessions when price pressures ease. During deflations the price falls, because the value of the dollar increases. But if financial institutions begin failing more quickly, particularly combined with falling investments of virtually all other types, people will again turn to gold for safety.

Should the U.S. or any other government return to even a partial backing of their currency by gold, the price must skyrocket. What is left of Russia could take the lead in such a development. Their ruble is worth little outside the country. By partially backing the ruble with gold, it could again be used for international commerce. Russia is also among the world's three largest gold producers. In such an event, to back the ruble, massive new supplies would be removed from the market and held in reserve, thereby sharply increasing prices.

When their backs are up against the wall, countries sometimes make it illegal to own gold—which the U.S. has already done in this century. In fact, this probably had much to do with the lack of interest in owning the metal until the late 1970s. Many feel ownership is still unpatriotic today. Of course the government downplays the importance of gold, because they want nothing to serve as an anchor to their ability to increase the money supply. Should a recall again be demanded, I would personally not comply.

In the case of gold mining companies, however, one's ownership is not as private. Should the government take drastic measures such as forbidding ownership of gold, one must at least consider the possibility of nationalization of gold mining companies. As such likelihood increases, investors should simply start diversifying into the shares of mines in other countries...even South Africa. I have worked and lived in that country for two years, and believe peaceful change is probable. But what might happen is still more important than what will happen. And investors can become fearful. This is why investors might wish to only buy gold mining companies outside of South Africa until political developments there become more predictable.

It should also be remembered that the U.S. has really never touched their gold supply in Fort Knox. On the other hand, they no longer have a silver reserve. So I would not be surprised if at some point in the future even the United States would again partially back certain types of "money" in gold. The most obvious choice would be actual circulated currency and treasury bills. And perhaps a new type of treasury bond. With the security of a gold-backed bond, the government would have to pay negligible interest on such issues, particularly in a deflation.

Compared to other markets, the gold market is quite small. This includes the market for gold mining stocks. So any increased demand, and particularly a flight to safety, would force the price of such securities into the stratosphere.

The share prices of gold mining stocks naturally reflect changes in the price of gold itself. But price volatility is largely a function of *production costs*. For example, if a mine is a high cost producer, the cost of production might be $350 per ounce. If gold increases in price from $400 to $500, their profits per ounce of production will increase from $50 to $150. So shares might be expected to increase up to 300%, with only a 25% increase in the price of gold. This is the case with most companies except South African and older Canadian mines.

On the other hand, a low-cost producer, such as the latter, might have production costs of only $250 an ounce. In the same scenario, their profits would only increase from $150 to $250 an ounce. So one might expect only a 67% rise in share prices for low-cost producers in this example.

Investors have four reasons for buying gold mining stocks:

- Appreciation (buy low, sell high)
- Inflation Hedge
- More liquid and more leveraged than gold itself
- Late Deflation Hedge

As a rule, gold mining stocks pay very low dividends. But in terms of appreciation, gold stocks certainly provide potential. Prices can move dramatically higher or lower with an associated move in gold prices. Because of this, many people consider them unsafe. As discussed before, don't confuse volatility with safety. Would you consider a company that literally mines true money as unsafe?

Everyone by now is aware of the role gold plays as an inflation hedge. The same is certainly true for gold stocks, particularly with their greater leveraging.

It is easier to buy and sell gold stocks than gold. Storage problems and the associated costs do not exist. Buying and selling is just as easy as for any common stock, particularly for small amounts of investment funds.

❖ *Focus and Courage* ❖

Most people are unaware of the potential of gold and gold stocks during a deflation. If the rest of the stock market, most bonds, real estate, wages, and prices are falling, how do you invest your money? If the safety of government bonds becomes suspect, what do you do? The only safe haven could well be gold and gold stocks. What would you use for money, if your bank is ready to close its doors? What is dependable money—pieces of paper, computer numbers? During such periods people inevitably return to the oldest and most reliable form of money in the world—gold.

It would be instructive to know how gold mining stocks behaved during the last deflation. Homestake Mining is one of the largest such companies in this country. Figure 3 shows that Homestake share prices increased six-fold in price during the 1930s. Including extremely high dividends, particularly if reinvested, investment values rose about ten-fold. Two factors were at work. Gold, then a monetary metal, could only be sold to the U.S. Government, who increased the official price by 69%. Secondly, deflation decreased production costs. This is an ideal combination for any company—lower costs and higher product prices.

During the next deflation, I fully expect the same developments. As labor unions now play a more important role, costs will again fall, but perhaps not to the same degree as during the 1930s. The price of gold is now determined by the free market, not the U.S. Government. So during a massive flight to safety, prices would be subject to an increase far greater than 69%. Particularly if gold resumes its role as true money, we could see $2000/ounce.

Gold mining stocks play an important investment role when inflation or deflation is a potential problem. Over the next four years, gold-related investments will probably experience a period of decline. This will be during the phase in which investors suddenly realize inflation is not the problem. Those who don't understand the stability of gold-related investments will probably sell. After all, isn't gold an inflation

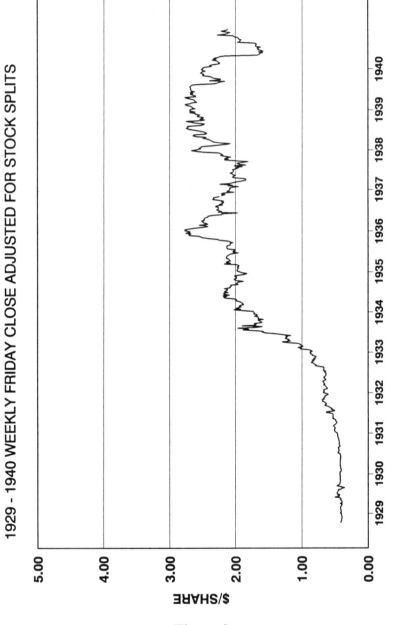

Figure 3

❖ *Focus and Courage* ❖

hedge, and nothing more? But as the deflation worsens, as the value of most investments plummet, as financial institutions start closing even more quickly, and as the prospects grow of governments again backing their currency in some way with gold...the value of gold and gold mining stocks will again be realized, and prices will soar.

This area represents a way to increase four times the value of our investments over the next four years. If remonetizing occurs (currencies are again backed by gold), the potential is ten times plus. In a 3-to-1 deflation, total purchasing power increases 12 and 30 times respectively.

Real Estate

Discussion of this investment is extremely important, because the buying or selling of a property is often the greatest investment decision most people ever make. I am therefore amazed at the casualness of so many people in buying a house or condominium. The potential for gain or loss is enormous.

Of course many people don't consider the purchase of a house an investment. But is this really true, particularly in the face of a real estate agent implying 5-10% yearly appreciation? This might have been the case over the last thirty years, but those expecting the same over the next four years will have a rude awakening.

Since entering the investment advisory business full-time in 1980, I've always been extremely careful about real estate recommendations. This is because it's first necessary that clients decide whether they are buying a house as an investment or a choice in lifestyle.

As a choice of lifestyle, buying a house has certain advantages and disadvantages. The advantages over renting are that you have full freedom in changing, fixing, repairing, and remodeling the house and surrounding garden and property. To a large extent, you can clutter up the place, not worry about esthetic damage, and make as much noise as you want. You are free to have pets, and let them roam anywhere they want.

And you don't have to worry that the owner will sell the property, forcing you to move. You also have more flexibility in choosing the exact neighborhood you desire. In addition, you can write off interest and property taxes on your tax return.

The disadvantages are that you must fully insure the property, spend the time and money to make or arrange all repairs, mow the lawn yourself, and pay real estate taxes, even if it's fully paid for. But most do not pay cash for a property. Few can afford to do so. Even if you could afford it, society and your accountant tell you it's cheaper to borrow so you can write off the interest on your income taxes. Other disadvantages compared to renting are the lost opportunity costs on your down payment (the money could be growing with other investments), and having to come up with the same mortgage payment every month, even if rent prices and home prices plummet, whether you still have a job or not.

So is your decision to buy a house a choice of lifestyle or an investment? Usually the decision is some combination of both. If it's primarily a choice of lifestyle, and you can fully afford it, current economic conditions suggest paying cash and owning the property free and clear. But if the purchase is for investment, and the possibility of rising prices constitutes more than a casual consideration, you could be making the greatest investment error of your life in the 1990s. This is because the price of everything rises and falls, sometimes over short periods, but particularly over periods of approximately fifty years in length. And we are now headed into the down phase for real estate.

I know what you're thinking. "But my house has skyrocketed in price since I bought it, my monthly payments are puny, and even then I can write off some of the payment on my taxes." Or, "I've become a millionaire investing in real estate, and you call it a bad investment?" These are the exact same terms used in the stock market of 1929 and 1987, and until it started crashing, in the Japanese stock market. Nevertheless, there was a period of some thirty years when it made sense to borrow, and heavily, paying off debt with ever-cheap-

❖ *Focus and Courage* ❖

er dollars as inflation forced prices ever higher. And this approach was often the most important factor in increasing people's financial worth during that period. But that honeymoon is over. The past is dead. From now on the rule is: "Pay off your debt, and fast. Move your money into those few investments that will do the same in the future as real estate did over the last thirty years." Paying off debt in a deflation when the value of the dollar turns around and starts increasing in value will become a nightmare.

The comment I hear most often is "It can't happen in our area! We've got Bigbucks International here, tons of government workers, thousands of military retirees, military bases, or this beautiful ocean vista." It doesn't matter. In fact, the same words were uttered over the last fifteen years in almost all other parts of the country, and it didn't help a bit. Virtually all areas of the country have experienced 20% declines in real estate prices during some period over the last fifteen years: The Midwest, as agribusiness deteriorated or large local companies saw their business decline; the Northwest, as lumber became only another commodity; the South, as oil prices tumbled from their lofty levels; Florida and the Southwest, due to massive over-development and a slower economy. Alaska has experienced declines of 40%, and the Northeast is still under pressure. Even New York City is seeing price declines (and big, smart money is even disposing of such institutions as Rockefeller Center). Even California has now experienced price declines well in excess of 25%. Commercial real estate prices are experiencing crushing declines almost everywhere, as banks often refuse new loans. Properties have been purchased from the Resolution Trust Corporation (the Washington entity responsible for disposing of S&L assets) for less than 20% of their cost of construction.

And remember, the above problems have occurred even without actual deflation (a negative Consumer Price Index). The process is only starting. And I can think of no local area that is impervious, provided credit has been used for purchases and as long as dollars are used to measure the price.

The greatest reversals tend to occur in areas that have seen the most lofty appreciation. In Southern California, for example, many 3-bedroom houses sell for $400,000. In Sacramento, the same house might go for $130,000. In rural areas, like parts of Nebraska, a similar house might sell for $10,000. Where is the most insanity? Which areas might you expect to experience the greatest tumble?

Some people say I'm negative on real estate. This is untrue. I'm simply thoroughly convinced that deflation is unavoidable over the next four years. And to determine what will appear to fall the most in price (due to the dollar increasing in value), I simply look for what the most people have bought with debt, and which market people believe will never fall. In 1929 that was stocks. Today it's real estate. If you own your home free and clear, you'll feel nothing, provided you can still afford to pay your taxes. (In the 1930s, when real estate fell only 50% in price, many people lost their fully-owned homes because they couldn't pay the taxes.)

As you might guess, I'm not very popular among some real estate salesmen. I really don't understand this. Properties will continue to turn over, perhaps more quickly than they do today. Salesmen will continue to earn their commissions. But if you're an agent whose success has been based on promises of virtually-guaranteed higher prices, you'll have to change your tune. If you're a good real estate agent, you will prosper.

Let's take a close look at how deflation affects real estate. You buy a $100,000 property for cash. In a deflation that only takes us back to the dollar's value in 1970 (we will probably go further), prices will seem to fall by two-thirds. In fact, the dollar has simply tripled in purchasing power. Your house is now worth $33,000. You're not affected, because your purchase did not involve debt. If you sold, those dollars would buy three times as much, so you have the same total purchasing power as today. But could you write off the "loss" of your home sale on taxes? Some might be surprised, but no, you can't.

But let's say you put 10% down and finance $90,000. Your

❖ *Focus and Courage* ❖

monthly payments are $800. In a 3-to-1 deflation, your property "falls in price" to $33,000. Wages and salaries also return to the levels of 1970. For monthly payments, this is the exact opposite of what happened over the last twenty years. They don't change. But instead of three times easier to pay, they become three times more difficult. That $800 a month now "feels" like $2400. And the value of that $90,000 loan balance feels like a quarter million dollars.

Doesn't this sound familiar? Do you remember our discussion of commodity futures at the end of Chapter Four? If not, please go back and review that section at this time.

You probably felt futures were too risky an investment. But in terms of investment leveraging, what is the difference between paying 10% down and controlling $100,000 of wheat or kryptonite futures and buying a $100,000 house with 10% down? Please tell me the difference. The most important dissimilarity is speed. With futures, you can lose or double your original investment in one week. With real estate, it simply takes longer. With real estate you don't encounter margin calls. But with futures you don't have monthly payments either. So this particular difference becomes a time-delayed wash.

Any other difference is denial. When you buy real estate with debt, *you are buying a real estate futures contract*.

But there remains two important arguments on behalf of real estate ownership. The first: "When you buy, you're at least growing your equity in the house." This is not true for perhaps 85% of home purchases. What normally happens is as follows. Young people buy a home as soon as they can scrape up the down payment and barely meet monthly payments. "Inflation will increase our wages." But within seven years, most either decide to trade up into a larger house, or get divorced (50%). The house is then sold. Over the first several years, virtually all monthly payments are interest only; there is no equity growth. They have paid perhaps $6,000 in sales commissions. The only increase in equity is if the home has increased in price. If another house is purchased, any equity generally goes into the new house. But again, there is no real equity growth, because early payments are for interest. Homeowners can also be relocated by their company, and the process starts all over again.

Most "equity" ends up in that mystical number called market value. But it cannot be realized unless the property is sold and the money freed. And this must be reduced by income taxes owed on what is basically an inflationary gain.

The second, and most often heard, argument for home ownership is "I have to buy a house for tax write-offs." When inflation was pushing apparent prices higher on a yearly basis, this made a lot of sense. Now, however, tax advantages must be balanced against future price declines. Assume your payments are $800/month, and $714 goes to interest. The property is now worth $130,000, and you're in the 35% tax bracket. You can write off (714 x 12) = $8570 a year in interest. In a 35% tax bracket, this saves $3000 a year in taxes. This is equivalent to 2.3% of property value. It's little consolation to save $3000 yearly on taxes when the value of your most important asset is falling 10% a year ($13,000). This is now occurring in California, and the same trend will manifest in all other areas of the country where 80% financing is the norm.

I'm not suggesting you immediately run out and sell your house. Important factors to consider are:

- The amount of debt on your property
- How much real estate represents, as a percentage of your total financial worth
- The size and liquidity of the rest of your investments
- The size and security of your monthly income

If your monthly payments are quite small, you're faced with one disadvantage and one advantage. The disadvantage is you have a great deal of equity on paper that is subject to depreciation. The advantage is an attractive cash flow. If other safe and liquid investments could pay off remaining debt,

❖ *Focus and Courage* ❖

you're in good shape. If your home is paid off, you have no great reason to sell. It might be a bit greedy to sell now, and buy back at lower prices. But this is a very rare opportunity to hit a home run financially.

If real estate is the lion's share of your total financial worth, you might have a problem. If selling a real estate limited partnership or rental property would reduce your dependence on real estate as an investment, this would make more sense.

If you have no other money that could be placed in appreciating assets over the next four years, or that could be used as a hedge against falling home prices, you probably can't afford a home right now. Salaries and wages will decline in a deflation. But if you're a military retiree, doctor, etc., you might be able to maintain income. But even retirement benefits will likely fall due to a negative cost of living index. Exactly which jobs are truly secure in a deflation? Only time will tell.

Upon final analysis, you have five options with real estate:

- Leverage the property to the hilt, but be ready and willing to walk away from the property if necessary
- Pay off the debt, and become free and clear
- Sell and rent a nice place for a few years
- Hedge against falling prices with other investments
- Increase income from the property

By getting as much equity out of the house as possible, you can develop money to invest in those few areas that will do well in a deflation. But this can make monthly payments particularly difficult. You must always be ready and willing to walk away from your property if your other investments don't eventually allow repayment.

Most people can't afford to pay off their mortgage loans. But it should be your first financial objective.

Selling will free investment capital over the next four

years, and allow you to repurchase at bargain basement prices. Very nice rentals are available. In some cases the monthly rent will be more than you're paying now in mortgage payments. But this is compensated by the cash received and its potential growth over the next four years.

Many people will find it emotionally difficult to sell their homes. One very practical solution is to invest enough in a deflation hedge, one that appreciates in price by the same amount your home value falls. Gold stocks or the longest maturity zero coupon treasury bonds are the most obvious hedges. But to do this, you must have other investment funds available.

Another option is to increase property income. This might include share rentals or converting the garage into an office. Either could involve some extra work.

An example might be helpful to clarify the opportunities in making the difficult decision to sell a house. Assume your home is worth $150,000 today, and your monthly payments are $600 against a $50,000 mortgage balance. You have precious few other investments and can't use a hedging strategy. If you sell and rent, let's assume $1000 monthly rent for a comparable home. Proceeds from selling are $100,000. After capital gains tax and commissions, you pocket about $60,000.

Investing in those areas most appropriate during a deflation should allow you to multiply that sum 3-4 times over the next four years, after subtracting the additional monthly outgo for rent. This would produce $140,000 to $190,000 by 1998. The same home, in a 3-to-1 deflation, could then be bought for $50,000 cash, still leaving at least $100,000, which would also have 3 times the purchasing power by then ($300,000 in today's dollars).

Using the same example and being much more conservative, let's assume only a 2-1 deflation (house prices only fall by half). You would only need a 16% annual return on your investment to buy the home for cash and be mortgage-free in four years, and still have $50,000 in today's purchasing power left over.

Options

Options did not pass our investment screen. But given the huge price movements in all markets over the next few years—most of them down—such securities offer enormous potential. This is because put options appreciate in value when prices fall. Even many professional investors are in over their heads when using these investments. But if there is some way we can solve this problem, we can't avoid looking at options. So let's find out how they work.

Options are often used by real estate investors. The greatest secret to real estate profits, particularly today, is controlling, not owning, properties. When you have a purchase option on a property, you have the right to go in and make improvements or even rezone the property. After completing such work, you then buy the property, perhaps for immediate resale.

A call option is the right to *buy* at a certain price. You will pay a certain amount for that right. Assume a property is worth $100,000. You pay $1000 for the right to buy at $110,000 before a certain expiration date. Why would you buy such an option? You think prices will rise, because you see a special opportunity not realized by the owner. Why would the owner sell the option? Obviously for the $1000 which is his to keep. But maybe the owner doesn't think prices will rise, or doesn't see the opportunities you do. You go in and make certain improvements or rezone the property, increasing its value. You then exercise your option, and buy the property which is now worth much more. You might then immediately sell it for a quick profit.

A put option is the right to *sell* at a certain price. It is not commonly used in real estate, but is common in other markets, particularly stocks. You buy a put option on a stock for $1, giving you the right to sell it at $90. It is currently selling for $100. You must exercise the option, or more commonly sell the option to someone else, before the expiration date, or it expires worthless.

The stock price drops to $80. You now have the right to sell something at $90 that's only worth $80. That means the price of your option will rise to at least $10, plus some amount because the stock could fall even further before expiration. You've turned $1 into at least $10 for every option owned.

Why would someone want to sell you this right (which is called option writing)? First, for the extra income. He is also probably confident the price of the stock will not fall by much, particularly as far as $90 within a short period of time.

In practice, options are sold in blocks of 100. So for the above option, 100 shares would be involved. You would have paid $100 plus commissions, and sold it for more than $1000, less broker's commission.

The components of an option are:

- Strike price
- Expiration date
- Option price

The strike price is the price at which the option can be exercised. It has nothing to do with the stock's current price. In our example this was $90.

Expiration date is the date the option expires. Any time before that date the put option buyer can exercise the option or (in most cases) sell the option to someone else for what the market decides is a fair price. Newspapers will list the option month. If the option is not sold or exercised by the third Friday of that month, it expires worthless.

The option price is composed of two parts. The first is the exercise value. This is the positive difference obtained from subtracting the stock's price (in our example $100) from the strike price ($90). If positive, the option is called "in the money." If negative, this value is zero, and the option is said to be "out of the money." When we bought, the exercise value was zero ($90 - $100, a negative), and was "out of the money." When we sold, this amount was $10 ($90 - $80), and our option was "in the money" by that value.

❖ *Focus and Courage* ❖

Another component of the option price is the time value. An option will obviously be more expensive if it has several months before expiration. Conversely, the time value will be smaller if near expiration. Although most people call the total option price the premium, I think of time value alone as the premium. It will also be much larger when the market is very volatile, and smaller when the market isn't expected to move much.

One can also buy call or put options on futures contracts, or on various market averages. For example, the Standard and Poor's Index of 100 stocks is a quite liquid market which we often use. In this case, instead of a specific stock price, the S&P 100 average is used.

You might think the above example of a stock falling by 20% unusual. On October 19, 1987, this size of move was exceeded for most stocks in a single day. In fact, one could have bought a November put option at a strike price of 285 on the S&P 100 for 3/8 (times 100 is $38) in early October. At that time the average was at 321. A few days after the crash, that same option rose to a price of 60 (times 100 is $6000), as the average fell to 244. So excluding commissions, the value rose by a factor of 150. This was a unique period because the market hadn't been very volatile, few people expected prices to fall, and the magnitude of that one day move was unique. That type of opportunity will probably not be repeated, but you should get an idea of the potential profits in this area.

This is a very difficult market to play for most people. The market must move far enough, and fast enough, in the direction you require, to at least exceed the time premium. And preferably much further. Over 80% of options buyers lose money.

This might appear to be a teaser. If this market is too complex for the vast majority of investors, why discuss it? There is a simple way to take advantage of this opportunity. For example, several of my clients got together and formed an investment club for very aggressive investment over the next few years. They then contracted my company to manage those funds. Minimum contributions are $25, and we allocated a maximum of 30% of total funds for investment in stock put options. In sum, this is one more way $1 can be turned into $10. In a 3-to-1 deflation, purchasing power of such investments could increase 30-fold.

No-Load Mutual Funds

Now that we have a good understanding of how stocks, bonds, gold mining stocks, and real estate really work, it's time to return to those investments that passed our investment screen. We found that by using no-load mutual funds for buying and selling these investments, we could eliminate sales commissions and redemption fees, obtain much higher liquidity, and in general simplify our investment program. But we haven't yet discussed how mutual funds work.

A mutual fund family is an investment company that creates various types of funds. In some respects they are like huge investment clubs. Money is received from individual investors, normally in minimums of $1000 (usually lower for IRAs). That money goes into the specific fund designated by the individual—for example, stocks, bonds, gold stocks, or a money market fund. Each fund then purchases the types of investments described in the prospectus.

The two greatest advantages of mutual funds over direct investment in stocks, bonds, and gold mining stocks are reduced commissions and diversification of interests. Simply buying a stock mutual fund gives you much greater diversification in that market versus the purchase of individual stocks.

To keep track of the interests of each investor, a beginning "share price" is set. It doesn't make any difference if this is $10 or $20. Your money will simply buy twice as many shares at the lower price. Every day the fund calculates the total value of its investments, which of course fluctuates daily.

The fund also has some expenses. Someone must determine what is bought and sold, people have to process orders

❖ *Focus and Courage* ❖

and keep the books, there are commissions when securities are bought or sold (generally in large blocks at very low commissions), and there are other typical office expenses. The fund also has certain advertisement costs to make investors aware of the fund. Expenses are deducted from the value of investments. With many millions of dollars in investments, or in some cases billions, such operating costs are a tiny percentage of your holdings.

The total net value is then divided by the number of investor shares outstanding. This is called the Net Asset Value. This is the price at which new investors will buy fund shares, or current holders will sell fund shares.

This method of arriving at Net Asset Value is for no-load mutual funds only. Some funds have an asked and bid price, because they charge an extra fee to purchase (a front-end load) or a redemption fee upon sale. This can be as high as 8.5% to buy, and is usually a lower percentage to sell. This money generally goes to sales commissions. This loaded fund pays sales commissions; a no-load fund does not. In fact, the only way to find out about no-load funds is by watching advertisements, through an investment adviser, or from magazine or book reviews of different funds. Of course a loaded fund also advertises, and generally spends more in doing so. There is *no correlation* between the sales commission (or load) you pay and a fund's performance.

I only recommend no-load funds. As long as you can find no-load funds that fit your investment needs, and we will help you do this, there is no reason to pay someone commissions. With these preferred types of funds all your money goes to work, and you pay nothing to redeem your fund shares. Particularly in the case of bond funds, we find it ludicrous to pay an 8.5% commission, which can be more than the first year's interest.

So we put our money into mutual funds of a particular type and forget about it, right? Wrong. We don't do this for two important reasons.

First, most people think that just because they're in a mutual fund their investment is "managed." This is true, but only in terms of which specific stocks or bonds are purchased and held. You are still at risk if stocks or bonds decline in price. Some funds try to increase the percentage in cash during market declines. But this can actually be a contrary indicator. When mutual funds' percentage cash is high, one is normally near the bottom of a market, and when cash is low, one is near the top in prices. It should, of course, be just the opposite.

Second, most mutual funds are "fully invested" at all times. That is, they keep a certain percentage aside in cash for potential redemption by fund investors, and keep the rest invested. This means that if you're invested in a stock fund, and the stock market declines, so will the price of your fund shares. The best example of this was October, 1987, when stock funds were hit as hard as most stocks. If you're in a bond fund, and interest rates rise, the value of your fund shares will decline.

So it makes sense to buy mutual funds when prices begin to rise, and sell when a market decline is beginning. Use the same strategy you would when buying and selling anything else.

Real Estate Investment Trusts function very similarly to mutual funds. Their greatest advantage over direct purchase of real estate is the increased liquidity. You can buy and sell such investments very easily.

Mutual funds also play an additional role in greatly simplifying financial planning. In years past, counselors always asked investors "Do you want growth or income?" By using mutual funds, such an analysis is no longer required. This is due to their superb liquidity. All one has to do is invest his money in the most sensible and timely of such funds. If you want growth, you won't have to touch such investments. If you want income, you can easily access needed money at any time, with the ease of simply writing a check. You can also arrange to automatically receive a set amount every month.

Money Market Funds

Money market funds are just like any other mutual fund. They differ only in the types of securities that are bought. They purchase short-term interest-bearing investments. Because these securities are short-term, it is uncommon to have any capital gains or losses. This allows the share price to remain constant at $1, with interest either sent to the investor, or reinvested to buy more shares.

During chaotic markets it is, however, possible for share price to decline. The most likely cause would be default of held securities.

The vast majority of money market funds buy CDs, commercial paper, bankers' acceptances, and sometimes overseas paper. Some called government money funds buy primarily government agency paper and treasury bills. A precious few government money funds buy nothing but treasury bills. The latter, because of growing deflationary pressures and increasing debt defaults, are among the only money funds I currently recommend.

A very interesting attraction of most money market funds is that you have check writing privileges on the account. This provides ultimate liquidity. Most have restrictions, however, on the size of checks you can write. $500 minimums are typical, and we prefer those with only $100 minimums.

The most common mistake investors make in choosing a money market fund is to pick those paying the highest interest rates. Some newspapers even regularly feature those yielding the highest returns. This has not created a problem so far, but remember: The higher the interest rate the higher the risk. The safest funds will pay the lowest interest. But even then, there is not a great difference in rates—certainly not enough to jeopardize safety.

Keep in mind that money market funds did not pass our investment screen, primarily because of poor growth potential. By the time you subtract taxes on interest paid and adjust for the inflation rate, perhaps only a 1% real gain is realized. We do not, therefore, consider money market funds as appropriate investments per se. But they are wonderfully liquid investments in which to park your money when other investments are not timely. So while you are waiting for a market buy signal in another area, you are collecting current interest rates.

Most mutual fund families have a stock fund and a money market fund, a few have a treasury bond fund, and fewer still have a gold mining stock fund. It is therefore important to choose a family of funds that offers all the appropriate funds you will need over the next four years. Two have been found to meet such requirements, and these will be presented shortly.

7

Your New Strategy

*To be what we are, and to become
what we are capable of becoming,
is the only end of life.*
         —R. L. Stevenson

IT IS ALMOST time to set aside our old investment belief systems in favor of approaches that are more appropriate. But two things must be done to allow us to move forward in confidence.

First, we will review how the investments we have identified generally move in price during the 50/60 and 7-year investment cycles. By combining the two we will know which areas have the greatest probability of rising in price during any period. This will affect the maximum percentage of our investment funds we would want to commit to each. We will also describe a system for knowing which particular day we should buy and sell each to further improve our results—maximizing gains and minimizing losses.

We will then name the specific investment vehicles to use. In other words, which mutual fund family is most appropriate for our new strategy. We will then bring everything together in a simple but effective investment technique.

The Big Picture

You are now familiar with how the 50/60 year business cycle works. In Figure 4 we can visualize how the three major markets have been moving during such a period, *when adjusted for inflation*. (Real estate tends to follow the inflation rate, with high correlation to real stock prices.) Notice that adjusted for inflation the stock market has *not* reached the high of 1966. We can also project the most likely moves over the next few years, for cycle completion.

Please note that these charts would also approximate the price movement during a cycle in which hyperinflation occurs (massive inflation rates). But because they are adjusted for inflation, the same trends would manifest.

It appears the last long wave peaked in 1974, which was shortly followed by a brutal primary recession. You may wish to again refer to Figure 1 in Chapter Three. The economy has appeared to rebound since then, but adjusted for inflation neither most commodity prices nor other markets have achieved new highs. In all but a few remaining pockets, real estate has done the same. Like the hamster in its exercise wheel, we've been running faster and faster since 1974, and going nowhere.

Since 1976 we've been experiencing a period of "false prosperity" disguised by inflation and frantic debt accumulation. In 1980 the back of inflation was permanently broken for this cycle, and the treasury bond market reached a long-term bottom. Gold spiked to a new high the same year and has since declined.

The U.S. stock market was the major recipient of a rising money supply in the 1980s, but is now struggling (particularly when adjusted for inflation). But Japan is now the world's major economic engine. Their stock and real estate markets (and California real estate) began their meltdown in 1990. So 1929 corresponds with 1990.

The obvious conclusion is the 54-year cycle peaked in 1974, but the most climactic phase of the downturn, which

❖ *Your New Strategy* ❖

Deflation Cycle

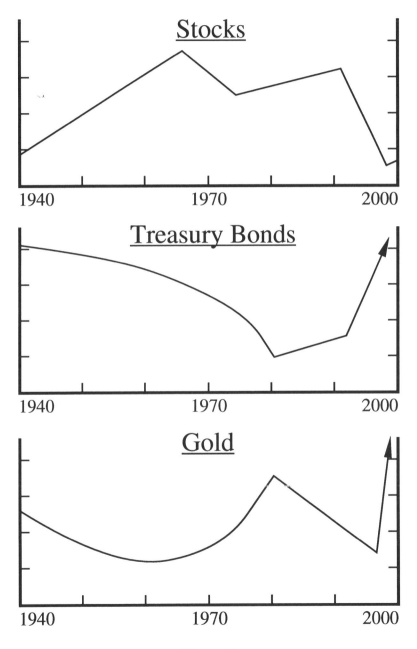

Figure 4

typically occurs about ten years later, was simply extended by one additional 7-year cycle. 1990 started the new worldwide deflation. These forces are now enormous, and will now pull our stock market down hard until about 1998.

Treasury bonds will remain in a long-term uptrend, with intermittent and perhaps sharp declines, until interest rates and deflation bottom, or the safety of government debt is questioned. The major factors preventing a major bull market in treasury bonds right now is concern over our growing government debt, a false fear of rising inflation, and high rates overseas. A falling dollar, against foreign currencies, is also aggravating the situation, making our bonds less attractive to overseas investors. Germany in particular might have to finish their 7-year cycle first and begin their recession, in order for worldwide deflation to begin in earnest. (Japan is already in full-fledged deflation.)

The gold market is not as clear-cut. Two major opposing forces are at work. Deflation will first try to force prices lower, and this pressure cannot be underestimated. When deflations begin, people sell assets of all kinds accumulated prior, to raise cash. Some of those assets could be gold. There are also too many investors who still see gold as only an inflation hedge. When deflation is obvious, we could see a sharp sell-off in gold. We are not ruling out a plunge to $150/ounce, before an epic and massive price rise. Investors will finally accept gold as a deflation hedge as well, it's only a matter of time. Other forces are acting to push gold prices higher: Its eventual attraction as other markets plummet (particularly the stock market); a safe refuge as financial institutions fail; the potential of remonetization of the metal; and its classical definition as the ultimate money in a chaotic monetary period. So over the *intermediate term,* the most important factor to gold prices is the speed of this deflation in the U.S. If slow, gold will experience price pressures. If fast, and a financial panic ensues, prices will soar.

We have already discussed the recession cycle and how

❖ *Your New Strategy* ❖

Recession Cycle

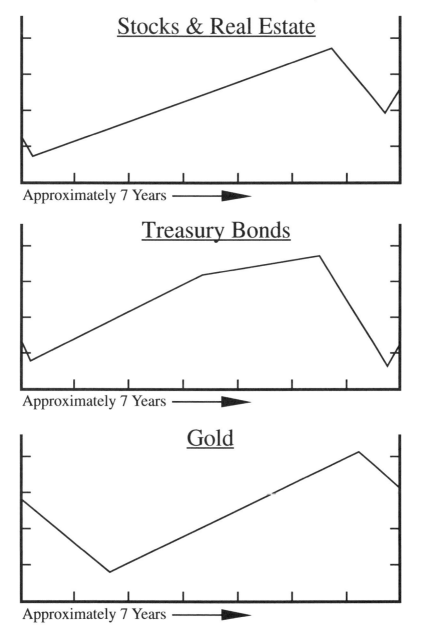

Figure 5

major investments move during that period. The charts in Figure 5 show the price trends for each.

We experienced a mild recession in 1990. The stock market responded with a nominal decline and has since made new highs (except when adjusted for inflation). In an economic recovery, interest rates are normally cut by the Federal Reserve Board. This occurred, and treasury bond prices rose sharply until October, 1993. Lower interest rates caused investors to expect higher inflation, and gold rose sharply in price in 1993.

In early 1994, the Fed became worried about strong economic growth and starting *raising* short-term rates to avoid a return of inflation. This was done despite the fact that no one could find any inflation in the economy. This caused trauma in all markets in 1994 and few investors made money in that year.

By combining the 50/60 and 7-year cycles, we can determine the most probable developments.

At the time of this writing, a recessionary recovery is near completion. But this is obviously not a typical recovery. Until recently, banks were stingy with loans, and preferred to buy treasury bonds. Most of the American public has gone on one last great borrowing binge via credit card debt, while those "in the know" are jumping off the debt treadmill. The last recession saw the permanent elimination of jobs, instead of layoffs, and this trend continues, even in recovery. Though unemployment is improving, many jobs are part-time, or at low pay, often without benefits. What is happening is the long term cycle is overpowering the recessionary recovery.

Higher interest rates in 1994 will impact in late 1995 or early 1996, forcing the economy off a sharp cliff. With the 50/60 year and 7-year cycles finally in concert on the down side, particularly in coincidence with overseas recessions, the worldwide deflation will become blatantly obvious. The stock market will start to move down in waves. On several occasions the bottom will seem at hand, and prices will rally, followed by another sharp decline. The Dow Jones Industrials

❖ *Your New Strategy* ❖

will not likely hit a real bottom above 1000.

The 7-year cycle is now placing downward pressure on bond prices, following a bond bull market. This should be temporary, particularly once the Fed suddenly realizes deflation, not inflation, is the real problem. High overseas rates will also temporarily push prices lower. But as worldwide deflationary forces gain momentum, bonds will move irregularly higher, with periodic large declines because of government deficit concerns. As the deflation deepens and the inflation rate turns negative, treasury bonds will experience price gains. At some point, even the direct obligations of the federal government will become suspect and treasury bond prices will collapse, but hopefully not default. With a terrible economy and plummeting federal tax revenues, the deficit will soar. At some point in time I expect the U.S. Treasury to back their bonds and bills with some percentage gold in Fort Knox, just to prompt investors to continue financing our debt. If this occurs, treasury bonds will begin an epic rise in price throughout the remainder of the depression.

With major opposing forces in place, gold mining stocks will experience large moves both up and down. As investors understand that inflation is dead, gold and gold mining stocks could even experience substantial declines. But as the stock market begins to collapse, the banking system starts to undergo numerous failures, or one or more countries decide to again remonetize the metal, gold mining stocks will rise massively. Gold and/or gold mining stocks could eventually be nationalized, and those diversifying into non-U.S. mines will continue to reap the rewards.

WARNING: Cycle research indicates the deflation process will have been largely completed by late 1998. This does not mean, however, that it will necessarily take that long to occur. In other words, a financial crisis could occur at any time, and the deflation could be suddenly over in one week. This is possible because of how tightly-wound our financial condition is, and the incredible speed of worldwide communications and market developments. A catalyst would be necessary. This could be anything from a meltdown in the Japanese stock market (particularly as it affects Japanese banks, who do business around the world), a far-reaching executive order issued by the President of the United States (our President has incredible emergency powers), the failure of a major U.S. bank (perhaps due to derivatives or leveraged bond/stock investments), a very large earthquake in California, a major military move by China or a third-world country, the failure of a major credit card security (banks create securities from such debt and sell them), etc. With the severity and frequency of earth changes growing exponentially, and debt so great around the world, there are many events that could suddenly trigger the final end. The worldwide stock market crash of 1987 was perhaps a witness to how sudden and dramatic the final deflation can be. It is therefore very important to get your financial house in order now, because no one knows when such an event could materialize or how fast it might do so.

Secondly, this does not mean everything financial will return to normal after 1998. It will require decades before we again approach nominal current prices, especially for common stocks, real estate, and virtually everything but treasury bonds, gold and gold stocks. This means that "recovery" from this depression will not resemble a "V" shape, but an "L" configuration.

We will now use the information gleaned from combining these two major cycles for one very sensible and unique purpose. That is to determine our *percentage allocation* for potential investment in each of these areas.

With both cycles pointing down for real estate in particular, and with that market containing the greatest debt, we allocate no funds for such investment. In fact, this is the last reference made to the appropriateness of real estate investing in this book. If we can pay cash for a home, that's different. But over the next four years massive declines in real estate prices are to be expected.

With both cycles pointing down for the stock market, we

❖ *Your New Strategy* ❖

allocate no funds for that market. This is not expected to change through 1998.

For average investors, we currently recommend an allocation of 70% for treasury bonds and 30% for gold mining stocks. You can choose any percentage you want, even including stocks, in your specific application of this approach. But this does not mean you place those amounts in such investments and hope. No market moves massively in any direction without volatility. The objectives are to be in a market when risk is low and prices are appreciating, and to be out during declines, which can be large, with the goal of buying back in at lower prices. We have already seen what happens with "buy and hold" strategies.

This means that when each market is attractive, with a single phone call we move that percentage of our funds into no-load funds that buy those securities. When unattractive, we move the money back into our safe money fund (treasury bills). See the schematic below in Figure 6. These percentage allocations and even the investments involved will change in the future, as one market after another soars or crashes, and risk/reward factors change. Let's call this our Conventional Account.

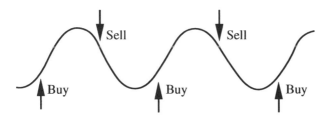

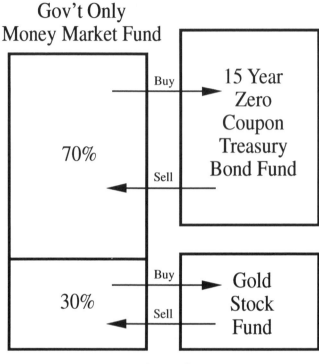

Figure 6

But we need a system for knowing exactly which day we should buy and sell each, which is the subject of the next section.

It might be appropriate to again comment briefly on the possibility of much higher inflation rates (hyperinflation). If this occurs, the value of bonds would drop dramatically as interest rates soar, and the price of gold stocks would skyrocket. The odds of this happening during this major cycle are virtually negligible. The major reason is a huge and sophisticated bond market. Should the inflation rate increase appreciably, a sharply-falling bond market would mean interest rates are increasing dramatically. Higher rates would shut down the economy within six months, still triggering the deflation.

❖ *Your New Strategy* ❖

Before proceeding it should also be mentioned that the simple action of stocks, bonds, and gold also tells us what type of economic period we are experiencing. This will help you refine percentage allocations into each area for your specific strategy, whether it be 1995 or the year 2010. If we can ascertain 3-6 month trends (adjusted for inflation) in the prices of each, we can use the following chart to determine what's happening:

Stocks	T-Bonds	Gold	
↑	↑	↓	7 Year waves, early inflation/reflation
↑	↓	↑	7 Year waves, late inflation; or hyperinflation
↓	↓	↑	7 Year waves, early recession; or financial panic
↓	↓	↓	Credit crunch, pending deflation
↓	↑	↓	50 year cycle, early deflation/depression
↓	↑	↑	50 year cycle, late deflation/depression
↑	↑	↑	temporary
↑	↓	↑	temporary

When To Buy And Sell

The investor who is successful on a consistent basis must understand four things very well:

- Which markets are the most attractive and most unattractive at any time
- How gamblers make money consistently
- Investor psychology
- Probability analysis

We have already solved the first problem with the help of the deflation and recession cycles. I'm often surprised at how many people work harder at being in rising markets than they do at avoiding declining markets. One must place equal weight on both.

Any investor would benefit greatly by taking some important pointers from professional gamblers. The first rule is to *never take all bets*. The professional gambler will never sit at just any table, or bet on every hand. He only commits his money when odds are in his favor.

He always evaluates *risk versus reward*. A winning gambler will seldom bet on the favorites. The payoff is simply too small to compensate for potential loss. He waits until he sees a development or opportunity that others don't sufficiently recognize. This is reflected in a potential reward that exceeds risk, particularly when several bets are combined.

The professional gambler *always has a system*. This is a critical point. He always knows exactly what he will do based on any development. This is mastery. While others ponder or try to make a decision, he confidently knows exactly what he will do in any situation. Without a system or strategy one becomes a victim of their own emotions, a reactor instead of an actor. What was your investment system?

The professional gambler is also *consistent and patient*. He knows that over a period of time he will be successful. He will accept some losses very easily, knowing that the big gains will more than compensate. He never panics because of this certainty.

Understanding investor psychology is also important. There are two types of unknowledgeable investors, the Wrong Way Corrigan and the Early Investor. Both arrive at the same psychological point.

The Wrong Way Corrigan waits before investing until everyone he knows agrees the investment is attractive. Once everyone thinks stocks, real estate, etc. are very smart things to buy, he jumps in. Corrigan also usually tells everyone of his decision; that he has done "the right thing." Of course by this time everyone who will buy has already done so. He pays top price, and the market heads lower.

Because his spouse and co-workers know of his purchase, they often ask how he's doing. When losses are small, the response is typically "It will head higher. It's only consolidating."

❖ *Your New Strategy* ❖

As losses become larger, the response is "I'm not worried about short-term moves, I'm a long-term investor." But deep down inside, Corrigan is seeking revenge. As soon as he can break even, and sell at his purchase price he will do so, sometimes waiting for years. This is the major reason why investments, particularly stocks, have trouble exceeding previous highs—all those Corrigans are waiting to "break even." But as prices move even lower, Corrigan will finally panic and sell. This is when all selling has been exhausted, and the market bottoms and starts back up again.

This might be a good time to remember our "100 of 100 survey" discussed in Chapter One. It might even be appropriate to go back and review that discussion at this time. Simply recall that when everyone thinks an investment will go higher, all money has already been committed. At that point there are no new potential buyers and everyone is a potential seller. The only possible direction for prices is down. So always avoid general opinion and common news. The crowd is always wrong. You must see something unique that doesn't include a lot of company.

The second category is called the Early Investor, who either by luck or various investment criteria somehow buys earlier in the move. As prices move higher the first psychological phase is greed. As paper profits mount, the investor becomes a bit omnipotent, knowing he can't fail. With such confidence, the investor becomes complacent, and seldom checks the price of his investment. Nothing can go wrong.

As prices peak and start moving down, however, psychology turns to hope. Such investors try to wish the market higher, but it doesn't work. As larger declines manifest, fear and worry start to set in. The final psychological phase is panic, and these investors sell. You guessed it. That is when the market bottoms.

To develop a good system we have to completely remove emotions from the decision-making process. Our objectives are two-fold. First, to be patient and not buy until potential reward exceeds risk. This will place us in that most enviable category of joining a *growing minority*. Secondly, we want to sell when everyone knows prices will head higher (everyone has already bought, and prices peak). The latter can be emotionally difficult, because few people will agree with you. You might feel quite alone.

I have studied hundreds of indicators, and kept the ones that work best. They seem to work because of four reasons. The first is an understanding of how the government tries to control the economy. They can no longer do this, but their attempts have certain effects the investor cannot ignore. Furthermore, we don't pay any attention to what the President or Federal Reserve Chairman says, but only to what they do. We are aware of which numbers to watch that reflect this.

The second requirement is a good understanding of how the international financial markets work. Having lived and worked overseas for six years, I understand well what happens in U.S. markets when our overseas friends make certain changes, or when their markets act in a certain way. This has created an international financial puzzle that fits together. When this changes, that is affected; when the Deutsche Mark falls, certain of our markets rise, etc.

The third reason is that we act on numbers not followed by most people, or we act on certain numbers before most people. You'll remember one of the important rules already discussed: "What everyone knows in investing isn't worth knowing." If we use the same numbers as most other people, we simply become one of the herd of lemmings.

Last, we've adapted some incredible technical tools to interpret the stock, bond, and gold markets. These are restricted and copyrighted tools purchased from the best investment advisers in the world. I am confident of these tools because extremely few people own them; they have an excellent track record; and because they were developed for and successful in the commodity futures market. Few people can argue that with the enormous volatility in all these markets, they are behaving much like commodity futures.

Without some familiarity with these indicators you will not

❖ *Your New Strategy* ❖

trust them. So let's review each. You will find they make total sense. We will only discuss those indicators you can reasonably understand, and of course only refer to those technical tools we cannot legally share with you.

Stock Indicators

FREE RESERVES We have already defined the Minimum Reserve Requirement. Free reserves is the amount of excess in the banking system above reserve requirements. This tells us whether money is "tight" or "loose." When this number is increasing, more stock investment money is available in the system, and the indicator is positive. When declining, or particularly if negative, this is a negative indicator for the stock market. We use a four-week moving average.

FEDERAL FUNDS RATE When banks have money above their reserve requirement (discussed above), they lend it to other banks who might be short. The federal funds rate is the interest banks charge each other for such loans. It is also the most sensitive free-market rate in the system. It can be used to anticipate increases or decreases in prime rates and often the discount rate itself. The trend in interest rates is important, because when rates are headed higher, heavily-indebted companies (virtually all) must pay more for debt. People will also borrow less, thereby buying fewer products and services from companies. The reverse is also true. If the federal funds rate is more than .5% above the discount rate (which is artificial and fixed by the Fed), particularly if rising, this is negative for stocks. If declining, or particularly if within .5% of the discount rate, this is positive for stocks.

STOCK OPTIONS By comparing the ratio of call volume to put volume, one can determine if there is increasing or decreasing optimism and speculation in the stock market. When this ratio reaches a high level, there is too much optimism and a subsequent decline is very negative for the market. When this ratio is not too high, but rising, stock interest is increasing and the ratio becomes a positive indicator for the market.

BONDS When indicators are negative for the bond market, soon to be discussed, this implies rising interest rates. This is a huge negative for the stock market. During a deflation, however, lower interest rates will imply not more eventual borrowing and buying by the public, but a terribly sick economy. So for this particular period, positive or neutral indicators for bonds is considered neutral for stocks.

ADVANCE/DECLINE LINE If one subtracts the number of stocks declining in price in one day from the number of gainers, you get an advance (if positive) or decline (negative). Regardless of what the Dow Jones Industrial Average does, this reflects what most stocks are doing. This is also referred to as breadth. By adding this positive or negative number to the previous day's total, and continuing a running total, we get an advance/decline line. When this line is increasing, most stocks are participating in an advance and this indicator is positive. When decreasing, most stocks are declining, and the indicator is negative.

OTHER TECHNICAL TOOLS Four other indicators were purchased from top research analysts, some for several thousand dollars, and are too complex to describe. Because they are restricted and copyrighted, I cannot even legally share them with you. Two are based on 8-day highs and lows for the market, and identify whether a reversal of prices is most likely a trend reversal or simply a short reaction before prices continue higher or lower. Two others are based on future price projections and whether the market is positive or negative. One of these is often neutral but periodically signals a major price move up or down, and has correctly anticipated many major moves, including the stock crash in October, 1987. Without these extremely effective tools, I would probably not even invest in the stock market.

The above factors form the core of our indicator system. We are constantly adjusting the weighting for each, and adding new factors, depending on overbought/oversold conditions, market conditions, and economic developments. The same holds true for the bond and gold stock indicators.

The Sentinel Index

We combine these indicators to issue a buy, sell, or hold signal in the following way. We first count the total number of indicators giving a signal (some can be neutral). We then count the number giving a buy signal. We divide this by the total and get a percentage from 0 to 100% which is SI, or the Sentinel Index, a proprietary index developed by my firm. If fewer than 42% are positive, the result is a sell signal. If 42-58%, it's neutral. A Sentinel Index above 58% is a buy signal.

Once an investor buys, SI's movement into neutral territory would be considered a hold. But the investor sells if SI turns negative. If an investor wants to go short, he would do so only when the index moves below 42%. The short would be covered on a move above 58%.

The Sentinel Index is calculated daily. How well does this system work? The Sentinel Index generates a buy signal when probabilities are well in our favor for higher prices. This means we will not participate in some market gains, but only the most attractive. Only buying when indicators are above 58% basically means that the probability of gains is approximately twice the probability of loss. Combining SI with the deflation and recession cycle analysis, we will usually not even have any funds allocated for a highly vulnerable investment. In terms of risk, the index has kept us out of major declines, and even for those periodic losing trades, the index has never kept us in a falling market long. On average we get three to four buy/sell (round trip) signals a year for each of the three markets.

When two of the confidential tools above are pointed in the same direction, the market will move in the opposite direction only 17% of the time. You might be curious what our indicators read before the October, 1987, crash. Free Reserves (for stocks) was the only positive indicator three weeks before the crash...a major sell signal. At the same time, no bond indicators were positive. That call was easy, particularly when seeing very poor numbers for stocks and bonds at the same time.

Bond Indicators

INFLATION Inflation has a massive effect on interest rates, as already discussed. But we don't wait for monthly CPI figures, which everyone receives at the same time. Instead, we follow the Commodity Research Bureau Futures (CRBF) index. If this Price Index is rising (moves above its ten-day moving average), this is negative. If falling, this indicator is positive.

TREASURY BILLS Uncle Sam borrows money at treasury bill rates, and lends money to banks at the Discount Rate. So by comparing the two, one can identify an insane, imbalanced monetary situation. Would you call borrowing money at one rate and loaning it out at much lower rates insane? If the 6-month treasury bill yield is more than .5% above the Discount Rate, particularly if rising, this is negative for bonds. If falling, and particularly if below a level of .5% above the Discount Rate, it is positive.

FEDERAL FUNDS See stock indicators, Federal Funds.

TWENTY-FIVE-DAY MOVING AVERAGE This is calculated for the no-load treasury bond fund used. When prices rise above the average, this indicator is positive. When prices fall below, it's negative.

COLAG This is an indicator obtained by dividing the index of coincident indicators by the index of lagging indicators. If down, the economy is slowing, removing inflation pressures, which drives bond prices higher. If up, the economy is strengthening and more loan demand and higher inflationary pressures will force interest rates higher and bonds lower.

OTHER TECHNICAL TOOLS We use the same four as with stocks, but against treasury bond futures prices.

Gold Mining Stock Indicators

THE DOLLAR When the dollar is becoming less valuable as compared against foreign currencies, it will take more to buy one ounce of gold. This appears as rising gold prices. The opposite is also true.

TWENTY-FIVE-DAY MOVING AVERAGE This is calculated for prices of the no-load gold fund used. When prices move above this average, the indicator is positive. When prices move below the average, it's negative.

MARKET COMPETITION A market tends to be more attractive when there is less money flowing into other markets. This particularly applies to the gold market, which is relatively small. Gold prices tend to move inversely to the stock market. When stocks are falling, gold tends to rise, and vice versa. When stock indicators are negative, this creates a positive indicator for gold. If stock indicators are positive, this is negative for gold.

OTHER TECHNICAL TOOLS Again, the same four confidential technical tools are also used for this market, and calculated against gold futures.

Investment hobbyists and semi-professionals will already have developed their own favorite set of investment indicators. With the plethora of computer hardware, software, and databases available today, systems can also be purchased. Many investment advisers also offer telephone hotlines and newsletters to assist in timing your buys and sells. Use such tools in combination with the strategy described for allocating percentages of funds into the most appropriate investments. This results in a core investment strategy for knowing when and what to buy and sell. You also now know which investments to use, and the ones to totally avoid.

But many investors don't want to devote the time and trouble to managing their own funds. Perhaps you generally use professionals for various purposes, want to stick with the trade you already know best, or just want to simplify your life. Many advisers will manage your funds for you. For example, my own firm, *Strayer Investment Advisers, Inc., offers three managed account strategies. They range from Maximum Safety for the most conservative of investors (retirees, for example) to Conservative Growth (for those seeking above-average gains), to Aggressive (for those seeking to maximize gains). The company always refuses to accept custody or possession of funds for client safety, and never sells commissioned securities, real estate, or insurance.

Mutual Fund Families

We now understand which investments make the most sense; how the long and short business cycles help us determine how to allocate percentages of our investment funds during any year; and how to know when to actually buy and sell. All we need is a specific vehicle for making those investments.

A no-load mutual fund family is that vehicle. What we want to do is first place our money in their government money market fund. When we receive a buy signal for stocks, bonds, or gold stocks, we instruct them to transfer the appropriate percentage into that fund. When we receive a sell sig-

*See Appendix

❖ *Your New Strategy* ❖

nal for that investment we instruct them to sell that fund, transferring the money back into the money fund. There are no fees, commissions, or even telephone charges for either move.

Over the years I've talked to dozens of mutual fund families, to determine which ones provide the greatest advantages. I used a very rigorous series of tests to determine which were the most appropriate for this strategy.

We prefer those that have all the following:

- A no-load common stock fund
- A long-term no-load treasury bond fund
- A no-load gold stock fund
- A money market fund that buys only treasury bills
- Check writing services on the money fund
- Low ($100) check minimums
- Small minimums for initial investment
- Small minimums for additions
- No switching fees between funds
- No restrictions limiting the number of transfers
- No custodial fees for IRAs
- Prices are available in most local newspapers
- Toll-free telephone switching between funds
- A phone system that works (few holds and seldom busy)

This is a demanding checklist, and the vast majority of mutual fund families do not qualify. Two come extremely close. Most fund families continue to add new funds and provide more services to investors. So we cannot be certain these are the only two such families, particularly as future changes occur.

Our first choice today is *The Benham Group. They were the first to offer money market funds for individual investors. They do not meet all our criteria, but the only shortfalls turn

*See Appendix

out to be inconsequential. *Benham restricts the number of withdrawals (sales) from their bond, gold, or stock funds to six a year for each fund, but our system has never generated more buys/sells than this number, so this is not a problem. This fund family is merging with Twentieth Century, but this will not change what follows, or related policies, except for the availability of more stock funds.

*Benham's money market fund, called Capital Preservation Fund, is most likely the safest money fund in the country. It buys only treasury bills.

Their Gold Equities Fund is well-constructed and provides good price movement.

Their Target Maturity bond funds are particularly flexible for more conservative and the most aggressive bond investors. They offer a series of zero-coupon treasury bond funds and you can actually pick the maturity in five-year increments. Maturity choices are the years 2000, 2005, 2010, 2015, and 2020.

*Benham offers two stock funds, which will be important at a later date.

Minimum purchases for any fund are low—$1000. One can make subsequent additions in amounts of $100 or more, either by check or transfer from another fund. They also charge no custodial fees for IRAs, which is obviously a benefit and quite rare.

You can write checks in amounts of $100 or more for expenses, mortgage payments...or simply to access your funds. The first fifteen checks are free, and additional checks are available at reasonable cost.

Your biggest decision with *Benham is choosing a maturity for your bond fund. The year 2010 zero fund will move in price about the same percentage as a 30-year bond. Shorter maturities will move less in price, and longer maturities will move more.

*Scudder Funds are our second choice. *Scudder was the first to offer a no-load fund many years ago. Capital Growth is their basic common stock fund. Their zero coupon treasury

*See Appendix

❖ *Your New Strategy* ❖

bond fund is available in one maturity, the year 2000.

They try to manage their Gold Fund, which generally results in less appreciation in rising markets and less depreciation in falling markets. This is a more conservative investment than Benham's gold fund.

U.S. Treasurys Money Fund is their safest money fund. But this fund carries a lot of agency paper.

Check writing minimums are $100, minimum initial fund investments are $1000, and no transfer fees are charged. Custodial fees are not charged for IRAs.

You might pose one typical question at this stage: "What is the past performance of each of these mutual funds?" With the major market changes anticipated over the next several years, we feel past performance is virtually unimportant. In fact, it is illegal for anyone to suggest past results are any indication of the future. Furthermore, particularly in the case of stock funds, the best performers over the last several years will most likely do the worst over the next five. And remember, we're not buying and holding, in which case such a question would be more relevant. All we want is a fund that is representative of the stock, treasury bond, or gold stock markets. By periodically buying and selling each we are basically trading the overall stock, bond, and gold markets.

It might also be appropriate to now address the practice of buying and holding, or as most brokerage companies suggest, "becoming long-term investors." I'm not sure why brokers suggest such a strategy. Perhaps it's to decrease stock market volatility; maybe it's to suggest that long-term stock investments are safe; or perhaps it simply recognizes that the average investor, without professional assistance, consistently buys high and sells low. Given the fact that most brokers are so new to the business, maybe they haven't even experienced a recessionary bear market. Perhaps they don't even understand how to adjust supposed gains for inflation. Or worse yet, they might not even understand deflation, let alone its great probability.

Regarding inflation, assume you "bought" the Dow Jones Industrial Average (which one can't do, but assume you could) in 1966. Further assume that group of stocks paid dividends of 4% a year. You invested dividends in a money fund paying 7% interest, and you sold your investment at the peak in prices before the 1987 crash. If your incremental federal/state tax bracket is 35%, as a long-term investor what would you estimate your total profits to have been? Adjusting for inflation and taxes on illusionary gains, your real return would have been a negative 2.4%. So much for long-term investing, which brokers inevitably recommend.

Numerous investment advisers have proven that even the most simple of common-sense investment strategies for periodically buying and selling can do quite well. By recognizing that all markets move in waves, and periodically buying near the lows and selling near the highs, incredible gains can be realized. This is the essence of our new investment strategy.

Summary

We now have a common-sense approach to determine what percentage of our investment funds we allocate to each of the major markets. But knowing that even major bull markets experience periodic and often large sinking spells, we also have a method for knowing exactly when to buy or sell each. The latter also serves as an important fail-safe system, should our longer-term projection of market trends be incorrect. We also have two mutual fund families that offer the required no-load funds for specific investment.

In the next chapter we will determine our personal investment objectives and goals. Some of us will be able to reach our goals by applying this strategy in a conventional manner. This will be done with investments that offer the least likelihood of major losses over the next five years. Such securities provide greater safety, growth potential, and liquidity than those investments you are likely using today.

*See Appendix

❖ *Your New Strategy* ❖

Let's call this our Conventional Account. If using *Benham, and using a Conventional Account strategy, this will involve Capital Preservation Fund, Gold Equities Fund, and probably their 2010 Target Maturity Bond Fund. I believe that using the above strategy with these funds can produce an average of 35% yearly gains throughout the remainder of this deflation. This percentage might sound a little high, but during the inflationary phase, stocks and real estate registered periods of very similar gains. And in a deflation, the inflation that developed over several decades is corrected in only a few years. In 1987 the stock market moved 22% in one day. That is a hint of the speed and magnitude of price changes in the future. This provides the opportunity of a three-fold increase after 1998 for the Conventional Account.

Some investors won't be able to reach their goals even with a three-fold increase. They might have no current funds, or their debts might far exceed their savings and investments. Welcome to a unique investment period that offers an opportunity for enormous gains. The *Benham 2020 zero bond fund offers a potential four-fold increase over the next four years, and Gold Fund should increase four to ten times. Put options offer massive growth potential in a falling stock market. But you might be in over your head in trying to trade most of these markets yourself.

One solution appears to be an investment club combined with professional management. For example, my clients formed a group called the River City Investment Club, a general partnership, for very aggressive investment. They then contracted my firm to manage these pooled funds. The minimum investment is $25. Some contribute the minimum, and others several thousand dollars. A maximum of 30% at any point in time can be invested in put options, and the remainder can be totally invested in the 2020 Benham zero bond fund or gold fund, whichever is positive, according to the Sentinel Index. The objective is to average 60% yearly gains over the next four years.

*See Appendix

The greatest gains will occur within short periods of time. Exactly when this happens, no one knows. In a 3-to-1 deflation, this would mean turning $1 into $20-30 purchasing power. Highest growth potential also means highest risk. But one would not expect more than a 50% loss in an absolute worst-case scenario. This would be appropriate for not more than 5% of total investment funds, and all the Found Money one can squeeze from their budget. For future reference let's call this alternative the Superfund.

8

Financial Planning

*He only is a well-made man
who has a good determination.*
—Emerson

          IN THE NEXT chapter we will actually begin our new strategy. We will reposition our current investments, and we even know where significant amounts of new investment capital can be obtained from our new budget. We know which investment vehicles to use and have sought out professional help to know when to buy and sell.

    But before we are truly ready and willing to put our new investment strategy to work, it's necessary to do some financial planning. What are your goals, your dreams, your objectives you want to achieve with an investment strategy? Once determined, and regardless of where you are now, it's then important to tailor your current resources to your personal application of the strategy discussed. This will help prevent those with significant savings and investments from taking bigger risks than necessary. It will also permit those who want to make up a lot of financial ground fast to achieve their objectives as well.

Goal Setting

It's now time to decide exactly what you want, and want truly. And this is no time to be shy in setting your objectives. The next four years will see the greatest transfer of wealth in this country's history. And it will occur rapidly. You now understand which markets will be the recipients and those that will experience vacuums, and why. This is a generational opportunity to achieve the loftiest of objectives and most of your dreams. During the last deflation some families generated enormous wealth, which even laid the financial foundation for electing a son President in the 1960s, simply because they understood what you have now learned and invested accordingly.

List your financial objectives, the things you want to buy, and the situations you wish to manifest by the end of 1998. There is one important rule, however: Specify the end result, what you want to do with the money, and not the dollars involved. For example, having $50,000 in the bank or doubling the value of current investments means nothing. This is because money is only one means for obtaining what you want. State your exact goals now.

_____

_____

_____

_____

Writing your objectives in this way first allows you to concentrate fully on their achievement. This will not only speed attainment of the objective, but will help you watch for means other than money for realizing your goal. Paying cash is only one way to get things. And discuss your objectives with oth-

❖ *Financial Planning* ❖

ers. You might find that another shares the same dream, and that you can help each other reach your objective, or share in the cost. You will sometimes realize that you can even trade something that becomes unimportant for something you do want.

Only after you have fully described what you want should you put a price on the item. Go back to your list and enter today's estimated price of each if you must pay cash. This will include such things as "Covering monthly expenses that are today $2000." Some things cannot be purchased, like "getting married." But a separate rough plan for achieving even this should be written, and this will involve certain expenses. For example, you might want to visit certain vacation areas, join certain clubs, or frequent various nice restaurants to meet potential spouses. All these things cost money.

Let's provide an example:

- Pay cash for a condominium. $80,000
- Cover today's non-shelter costs of $1110/month with the growth/interest on my investments without touching the principal. $268,000

Today's cost of these objectives is $348,000. If one can increase their financial worth sufficiently by 1998, the condo will be purchased for cash, and monthly income needs will be taken care of indefinitely. But if this cannot be afforded now, how much would we need today to reach these objectives, if funds were properly invested, without additional savings and investment capital? Assuming a 3-to-1 deflation, by 1998 these things would "cost" only one-third what they do today, or $116,000. Using the Conventional Account, which is not overly-aggressive, we can reasonably expect a tripling of current investment funds by 1998. So we would need one-third of the $116,000 today ($39,000) to reach our objectives without depending on additional savings or income. Or without being more aggressive than necessary.

If we have less than $39,000 today for this example, an appropriate amount would be invested in the "Superfund" to create the necessary gains.

This example should provide some important guidelines to determine how to write and "price" your objectives, if you are forced to pay cash for your goals. It also illustrates the future value of current investments or any cash or savings you can immediately develop from your new target budget. Of course one can always change their primary goals. But be careful when doing so to avoid the development of greed, which generally produces the "a little bit more" syndrome.

Certain goals appear time after time in people's lives. For example, most people would love to be totally out of debt and have their homes fully paid for, never having to worry about mortgage payments again. And who wouldn't like to have his basic monthly expenses covered from investment interest or gains, without ever touching the principal? I've developed an approach, called "The Apollo Strategy," for doing exactly this.

The following describes five financial categories with practical associated strategies for each. The Apollo Strategy also recognizes the vulnerability of most jobs over the coming period. You will find this strategy extremely helpful in tailoring a strategy just for you.

The Apollo Strategy for Financial Serenity

First estimate your basic monthly expenses, which you have likely done already. With long-term treasury yields near 7%, and assuming an average tax rate, multiply the monthly total by 260. Add to this amount your total long and short-term debt, including mortgages. Do you have investments worth this much? If so, pay off all debt, place the remainder into 30-year treasury bonds, and live off the interest. You have achieved Financial Serenity.

This assumes that the government will never default on its debt. This remains to be seen, given the still growing and currently-unparalleled level of government debt. Because of these

❖ *Financial Planning* ❖

uncertainties, you might want to consider having that amount managed by a company that fully understands the risks and opportunities of the next four years.

Additional finances and income beyond this amount could be committed in a multitude of different areas. The key would be timely diversification. It would make a great deal of sense to place a significant percentage of extra funds into bullion gold coins like Maple Leafs, storing them, and forgetting about them.

Having already achieved Financial Serenity, the primary emphasis is protecting one's backside. You are in a rare category and must protect what you've accomplished. Never compromise on medical insurance, and never purchase investments in which you can lose more than you invest. The latter includes leveraged real estate for about four years, commodity futures, and the writing of options (versus buying them). Owning your own business would also fall into this category, should losses start to consume capital instead of increasing it. Decide well in advance the maximum you will commit to a business before throwing in the towel.

Financially Vulnerable

95% of us are not in the above category. If not, the first objective is to protect ourselves against falling equity in our home, and to be in a position to fully pay off the home loan in 1998. It would be necessary to move about $350 into the Conventional Account today for every $1000 in mortgage debt to accomplish this.

If you cannot afford to do this, you might have some serious decisions to make. Or you can place $100-150 into a Superfund arrangement for every $1000 in real estate debt. If you still don't have enough, you are Financially Vulnerable and basically can't afford to own a home (a "real estate futures contract") right now. Or you must be ready and willing to walk away from your property if and when monthly payments become unbearable.

> A creditor is worse than a master; for a master owns only your person, a creditor owns your dignity, and can belabor that.
> —Victor Hugo

The Apollo Strategy for Becoming Shelter Secure

Let's say you can do this (invest sufficient funds to protect home equity) or already have your home paid off. (We will discuss renters in a moment.) Congratulations, you are now Shelter Secure. In four years you have the opportunity to own your home free and clear. Really owning your own home is a wonderful position to be in. This is because as much as 40% of one's outgo normally goes for house payments or rent. No longer having this expense will make your future income a real powerhouse in rapidly developing additional savings or investments, or greatly increasing your standard of living. Most people get divorced, move too often, or trade up into a more expensive home, and end up chasing rent or mortgage payments (mostly interest) all their lives.

The Apollo Strategy for Becoming Debt Free

You've now taken care of your shelter costs. Next, add up your other long-term debt and short-term debt, such as credit cards. After subtracting for shelter investment, do you have enough in your liquid investments to pay it off? If so place that amount into your Conventional Account and specifically label it "debt repayment." The principal would be reserved for debt repayment, and any excess (including growth on the debt repayment funds) can be used for other purposes like pursuing Financial Security (below). You've now graduated to Debt Free. Let's say you can't arrange to do so just yet. If not, use half of all the Found Money you can put your hands on against this debt repayment and place the other half into the Superfund. As soon as the balance in your Superfund allows total repayment of debt, you too graduate to Debt Free—even if you don't actually pay off that debt. Simply be certain not to incur additional debt in the interim.

> His brow is wet with honest sweat,
> He earns whate'er he can,
> And looks the whole world in the face,
> For he owes not any man.
> —Longfellow

The Apollo Strategy for Financial Security

After becoming debt-free, there remains only one final objective: Use the strategy to invest remaining funds so that after 1998 you can pay all remaining living expenses with the interest, dividends, and growth on a principal amount that is never touched. With your shelter costs and other debt taken care of, and for a moderate lifestyle, this requires placing about $30,000 today into a Conventional Account for every adult in the household. Add $14,000 for each child you will still be supporting at that time. If you already have such amounts, congratulations, you've reached Financial Security. If you're not there yet, place about 95% of your current investments in the Conventional Account, and the remaining 5%, plus any and all new Found Money, into the Superfund until you arrive.

Much of the above is designed to deal with current debt on a home. We haven't yet discussed those who rent. Your investment decisions are much less complex. You are also more flexible in taking advantage of enormous opportunities in the coming years.

First list all your long-term debt. Go back and review and use the same strategy used to repay mortgage debt ($350 in the Conventional Account, or $100-150 into a Superfund, for every $1000 in debt). If you can't do the latter, you have some serious Found Money to carve out of current expenses. If the end still isn't in sight, see ways to increase income in Chapter Ten. If a negative cash flow is driving you crazy and Chapter Ten doesn't provide some relief, bankruptcy might be an option. People certainly won't be interested in assuming more debt in the next several years, so losing a credit rating could prevent many people from making a difficult situation even more precarious.

Once we've arranged to cover long-term debt, renters would then total all short-term debt. Go back and review and use the same strategy as non-renters until you have become debt-free. And avoid additional debt.

The next objective is to be in a position to pay cash for a home or condo after 1998, or keep renting and pay for rent with the interest, dividends, and growth on your investment principal from that date forward. This would even perhaps be our first objective, because shelter is such a major percentage of total living costs. And to have this totally covered is a wonderful and free feeling. If you live in an average city this requires current funds of about $14,000 for a house for a man and wife (invested in the Conventional Account), or $9,000 now for a condo for a single person. This might sound like too little, but remember real estate prices will drop dramatically over the next few years, and your regular investments will approximately triple by then. It's even possible to use only about $6,500 or $4,200 respectively in a Superfund to achieve the same results—particularly if you can arrange to have your IRA accepted into the Superfund.

The current renter's final objective is to pay for basic non-shelter living expenses after 1998 with the proceeds from his investments from that time forward, without touching principal. This requires current funds of about $30,000 per adult and $14,000 per minor in the household, invested in the Conventional Account.

In other words, a man and wife who are now renting, and have no debt or children, need about $74,000 now, invested in Conventional Account investments through 1998, to buy a home for cash and cover all living costs indefinitely from that date on...without working thereafter. This is current Financial Security. A single person needs about $39,000 today to do the

❖ *Financial Planning* ❖

same, but buying a condominium instead of a house.

Keep in mind that this strategy, after 1998, assumes no dependence on Social Security income, retirement income from past employers, or even a job. This doesn't mean you won't have a job by then, or that Social Security or retirement plans will be bankrupt. Such incomes are simply wonderful bonuses. But expect major surprises. It's simply time for Americans to take full personal financial responsibility for their future; have a clear and professional plan for achieving financial serenity; and take advantage of an investment opportunity which occurs only once every 50/60 years.

Let's summarize the categories and what each mean:

Financial Serenity: Having the ability today to pay off all debt (including owning a home free and clear), and invest enough so that you can live off the proceeds without touching the principal investment.

Financial Security: Having the ability, today, to invest sufficient funds in such a way as to achieve Financial Serenity after 1998.

Debt-Free: Having the ability, today, to invest sufficient funds in such a way as to pay off all debt (including owning a home free and clear) after 1998.

Shelter Secure: Having the ability, today, to invest sufficient funds in such a way as to pay off an existing home mortgage or pay cash for a new home after 1998.

Financially Vulnerable: The precarious position of today not having enough funds to invest in such a way as to pay off long-term debt after 1998. This normally involves a real estate mortgage, and one might lose any equity and the property in the next four years.

Summary

The most important step in planning your financial future is to determine the current costs of what you want to achieve after 1998. But in the interim we must always be alert to ways of achieving those goals without cash, or with less cash, by focusing on our objectives. The following will help you tailor a highly personalized approach for their achievement if you must pay cash.

If one of your objectives is to cover your basic living expenses with the proceeds of invested funds from that target year on, first assume a moderate lifestyle. This will help you avoid the temptation of greed, and also assist in defining an objective that is challenging but readily attainable. Remember as well that you will have some income in the future, even though we're considering that a bonus. We assume that you can clear a 5% yearly after-tax return on invested funds from 1998 on, particularly if they are professionally managed, to use for living expenses. So take your basic non-shelter monthly living costs in today's prices, multiply by 12 for a yearly figure, then multiply by 20 (or divide by .05 for yearly return), and then divide by 3 (estimating a 3-to-1 deflation).

Next total your long-term debt, including the balance of your mortgage. This number *cannot* be divided by 3, because these debt values will not deflate. Add this to the above number.

Estimate today's price of any other objective. If you are a renter, state today's value of the property desired. As future purchases, you can divide this total by 3 (for deflation). Add the result to the other two numbers. This is the total amount to which you must make your money grow after 1998 for accomplishment. We'll call this your Target.

Next, total the current net market value of your savings and investments today, that you can quickly move into the investments recommended. Deduct any commissions or taxes due from sales. We'll call this your Current Reserves.

❖ *Financial Planning* ❖

You want your Current Reserves to grow to your Target in four years. We have two ways to get there. The Conventional Account should grow three times. The Superfund account should grow six to ten times. You can play with different ways of dividing your Current Reserves into the two areas to achieve Target.

The foregoing does not take into account two things discussed earlier in the different Apollo Strategies. The first is short-term debt. It is assumed this will be covered over the next several months with regular monthly payments (not Current Reserves).

Also excluded are your future additional savings, and money you can carve out of your budget (Found Money), and the gains on such amounts. These will also assist in arriving at Target. But depending on when these funds are made available, they will have less time to grow than Current Reserves. So their future value will be less, but far from unimportant.

You now have all the information necessary to develop your personal plan and become totally debt-free after 1998. This is due to a unique investment opportunity. In the next chapter we put it to work.

9

Financial Freedom

*Nothing of him that doth fade
But doth suffer a sea-change
Into something rich and strange.*
—Shakespeare

IT'S NOW TIME to amend our investment approach. We will lay aside our prior, less-effective approach, and adopt one that is more appropriate and timely. At the end of this chapter we will have repositioned our investments and put our new strategy to work.

We've come a long way in increasing our understanding of investing and have even chosen a strategy that makes the most sense for us. But we've gone into a lot more detail than many want or need. So it's critical at this point to make sure we don't lose track of the big picture. So it's imperative to summarize what we've learned so far.

We first discussed denial. We were surprised to learn how critical our financial condition is in this country. The government, companies, and individuals have amassed unparalleled levels of debt and much of it will not be repaid. We are even in worse condition than in 1929. The situation has reached critical mass.

We then discussed why we were not aware of these developments. One reason is that they've materialized so slowly.

But the major reason is due to vested interests. We're now very aware of the importance of asking ourselves if a person could have an ulterior motive for telling us something, or for recommending a certain investment. Or if a writer naturally represents a vested interest group. Here is the acid test to apply: If the person in question said the exact opposite, would they have anything to lose? Perhaps their job, a sales commission, or even an election?

Next we learned exactly how inflation and deflation work. We learned that debt is instrumental in producing inflation, and deflation is caused by debt liquidation. Very simply, inflation and deflation represent what's happening to the value of what we call a dollar. The measurement of anything in units that change will make it appear that the item being measured is changing. In some cases, particularly during inflations and deflations, the value of a product or service is even more stable than the unit of measurement, the dollar. We hope you will never again utter the words "prices going up (or down)," except when supply and demand are the only factors at work. And when anyone else mentions something like higher stock or real estate prices, or a certain interest rate or return, we must always ask "Is that adjusted for inflation?" You now have a better understanding of inflation and deflation than 90% of the population.

We then presented the 50/60 and 7-year business cycles, and exactly how major investments perform during each. In fact, everything in this world is based on a wave or a cycle: Birth and death, light and sound, sunrise and sunset, even the quantum physics that comprises matter. By applying these waves and cycles to investments and knowing where we are in each, we are placing understanding before experience. That is, we don't look for events where they won't be found. We don't place high probabilities on the leaves falling in the spring, or gamble on snow in the summer; or invest in real estate and common stocks over the next few years.

We next evaluated all major investments for safety, liquidity, and growth potential. During a volatile and dangerous economic period we cannot justify any investment that is not above average in all three areas. Just as cream rises to the top, four investments passed our test. These were no-load stock funds, no-load treasury bond funds, no-load gold mining stock funds, and Real Estate Investment Trusts. Although it did not survive the test for growth potential, we added money market funds that only buy treasury bills, to serve as a cash parking place when investment in the other four areas was inappropriate. Although put options did not survive the test, we added them as well, for the benefit of extremely aggressive investors who demand greatest leverage and profit potential to reach specific financial goals with limited funds.

Once our investment universe was reduced to only six common-sense investments, it was then possible to take a close look at each to see exactly how they worked. This vastly simplified our investment approach and increased our understanding of the most important securities.

By combining the deflation and recession cycles, we then determined which areas offered the greatest risk and the greatest potential over the next four years. Common stocks and real estate were eliminated. We found that treasury bonds and gold stocks were the most attractive. This same review also permitted us to determine what percentage of our funds should be committed to each when they offered the greatest probability of appreciation.

We also described how The Sentinel Index is constructed, which allows us to know when to actually buy and sell each no-load fund. Many investors spend certain amounts of money and vast amounts of time to figure out how to beat the markets. My company has already done this and we are making our findings available to you. We were fortunate enough to have the capital to invest many tens of thousands of dollars in the best tools and information available from the top investment minds in the world. My firm has also invested time—full-time for fifteen years—to carve out the true from the false. To this we've added many years of actual investment experience in all investment markets and six years of rare international experience to present you with a simple, complete, and effective strategy.

We then identified the best mutual fund families to use for these investments.

Finally, we discussed several helpful guidelines in determining your personal investment strategy. By comparing your goals with your actual resources, it was a simple matter to determine how conservative or aggressive to be with what percentage of your funds in order to reach Financial Serenity after 1998. A rare economic period provides the opportunity, and now you have all the tools. It's now time to put them to work.

1. Your Road Map

Confirm and concisely write your objectives. Then specifically state how you'll get there from the strategies described in the last chapter. Are you at the level of seeking Financial Security, or is your current task to be Shelter Secure? Briefly rewriting your objectives and plan sounds like five minutes of extra work, but it's easy in six months or a year to forget the big picture—what you're trying to do and how to do it.

Next, restate the total value of your current investments or available monies from your inventory in Chapter Four. What percentage do you need to commit to typical investment (Conventional Fund) and to very aggressive investment (Superfund), to reach your goals after 1998? State exactly how much you can currently commit to each area. There might be some investments that are totally tied up and impossible to access. Exclude them for now.

2. Decide On Professional Assistance

If the total of your liquid Conventional Fund money is more than $4,000, you might be eligible for a managed account. IRA minimums are less, at $2,000. Immediately upon buy/sell signals from the Sentinel Index, *Strayer Investment Advisers, Inc. appropriately transfers funds within your account for you. For your safety and peace of mind, we never have custody or possession of your funds, but only direct their movement. This arrangement includes an initial financial review and ongoing financial planning assistance at no extra charge. Financial reviews can even be conducted long distance, with the client submitting data in advance and culminating in a telephone appointment.

If you want to manage your own monies, or if the amount for your Conventional Fund is less than $4,000, you will want to seek out a professional investment adviser who can provide newsletters or telephone hotlines to help you decide when to buy and sell.

If you have less than $4000 today for conventional investment, you will have trouble using this method with a mutual fund family because of the $1000 minimum initial investment for the individual funds. An investment club makes the most sense for this amount. Again, seek professional help in managing club funds.

For your Superfund monies, an investment club with professional management is the best approach. *Strayer Investment Advisers, Inc. can assist in the formation of a club. It's a simple matter to start your own group. It's suggested you start by contacting the *National Association of Investors Corporation.

Decide which type of assistance you want to use, and make immediate arrangements to obtain details and begin that service.

3. Reposition Investments

Liquidate current investments for movement into your conventional and aggressive arrangements. This might be a good time to go back and review the discussion of each security pertinent to your situation in Chapter Four. But there are

*See Appendix

frequently special considerations in the sales of each, so we will briefly review them at this time.

Certificates of Deposit: After adjusting for taxes and inflation, one realizes less than 1% real yearly return. This simply does not compensate for risk, given the rapidly mounting banking/S&L crisis and an FDIC with extremely limited funds. And given government debt, don't count on eventual support from Washington. Upon sale, you will encounter another pitfall for this area—liquidity. Early withdrawal entails a penalty of 2-3 months interest. Suggestion: If the security has more than six months until maturity, take a deep breath and pay the penalty, in order to increase safety, liquidity, and growth potential immediately. If less than six months to maturity, you will be tempted to not liquidate early.

Money Market Funds: Some 95% of all such funds primarily buy commercial paper and CDs. So refer to earlier comments and remember the growing risk of unsecured company IOUs. Some people think of money funds as investments. We simply view them as temporary cash positions—but only as long as safety remains reasonable. They are, however, extremely liquid. So liquidation is very simple, involving only a redemption letter or the writing of a check.

Cash Value of Life Insurance: That's your money in the cash value, and you even have to pay interest to borrow it. First, make sure you maintain insurability (which means that you can't be turned down for additional insurance in the future because of health, marital/dependent changes, etc.) within a new term insurance policy. Make sure you're approved. Only then get the cash value out of current whole life policies and cancel them, even if you buy term insurance for the next few years only. This will also decrease premium outlays compared to whole life, putting even more funds into Found Money during that period. Invest the difference; don't spend it.

❖ *Financial Freedom* ❖

Insurance Company Products: This includes Guaranteed Investment Contracts, Universal Life, Annuities, and an endless list of other products, many of which include some form of insurance. You paid a healthy commission when you purchased, and will likely pay another upon sale. Grit your teeth and simply do it. You can do better on your own, without a middleman. If you can't self-insure, buy insurance, but always separate the investment portion.

Investment Real Estate, Trust Deeds, REITs: Real Estate Investment Trusts offer good liquidity. Simply sell them. They're not appropriate and will decline sharply in price over the next few years. Obtain for your trust deeds the best price you can, first contacting the person who sold them to you. If you own rentals, commercial or residential, you've probably been making most of your decisions based on rental income or expected appreciation. Both will become precarious, and your monthly payments won't budge an inch. You'll surely agonize over the coming tax bite upon sale, and your CPA's reaction will be even more pronounced...until he reads this book. Remember that the subsequent tax due never was your money. You might even be patiently waiting for a tax change that will make capital gains tax less obtrusive. Simply ask your CPA one question: "What percentage price decline in the property would wipe out all current or potential tax advantages?"

Your Home: Return now to the example on real estate in Chapter Six. Very simply, if you have a mortgage on your home, you have, in effect, purchased a "real estate futures contract." When prices are rising, for any reason, your equity on paper surges. On the other hand, when property values are falling, it will be the most sickening feeling you've ever experienced—unless you have actually traded futures contracts. One by one, homeowners who don't act early will even start to experience prices falling below mortgage values. This is called negative equity. It will sometimes appear that property prices are bottoming and starting to firm. You will sigh some relief, hoping the worst is over. Such events are typical in bear markets and deflations. You will have fallen into "long-term investor" syndrome. Of course the strategies discussed in the prior chapter do everything possible to assist people in keeping their homes. In sum, the decision to buy or sell must not be an emotional one, but based strictly on the size of mortgage debt compared with the level of other savings and investments. Also see tax comments in the prior paragraph.

Bonds - Municipal, Corporate, and Government Agency: Safety concerns will quickly move through the ranks of these issues, driving their prices lower. So simply sell them.

Treasury Bills and Treasury Bonds: Physical treasurys should only play a role in your strategy if you have already attained Financial Serenity, or are very close to it. Otherwise, make these investments at *Benham. Obtain the increased liquidity to periodically stand aside from the bond market when prices periodically decline—without paying commissions each time.

No-Load Funds at Other Institutiont The superb liquidity of this group becomes apparent when you move your funds from them. Simply call and transfer all monies into the money fund on which you have check writing. Call a few days later for your new balance, and write a check for that amount to Capital Preservation Fund at *Benham. There will only remain a tiny amount of interest not yet applied. Just call later and instruct them to close your account and send you a check for that small sum. If for some reason you don't have check writing privileges, call the mutual fund and obtain specific instructions on how to write your redemption letter. You might be tempted to try to use our strategy where you already are, simply because you're more familiar with the company. Breaking the rules now will lead to confusion later. And your fund probably doesn't have as many treasury bond choices as *Benham (or even *Scudder), a gold fund, or as safe a money fund.

*See Appendix

❖ *Financial Freedom* ❖

Without a super-safe money fund holding treasury bills, I can even envision someone, during a chaotic market, wanting to move money into a gold fund and not being allowed to do so. At such a time there would be a massive flight to safety into treasury bills. This is exactly the securities your new money fund holds.

Mutual Funds with Loads: You've paid a commission to buy, and might well pay a commission for redemption. Might that hold you back? Purchase commissions are money that's dead and gone. Even for redemption fees, you will have to pay them sooner or later. Do it now to get into the recommended no-loads, so you never have to worry about fees again. See previous paragraph on actual transfer if you have check writing privileges. If you don't, you'll have to write a letter of redemption. Call them to see exactly how to word it.

Individual Stocks: Sell immediately. The market is at enormous risk. You might have become emotionally attached to a certain stock. Perhaps you even work for that company. Or maybe you own stock in the most timely and attractive company in the market. It doesn't matter. When the bear attacks in earnest, he'll take the good girls with the bad. One acid test: Exactly how much did your stock appreciate or depreciate on October 19, 1987? At an absolute minimum, set a stop loss 5% below today's price. If it rises, raise the stop, but never, ever, lower it. But even if you place a stop loss with your broker, this is no guarantee. In a sharp move down, the market can cut through your stop loss like butter, and never trigger it. By not buying individual stocks in the future you will also pocket the commissions you would normally pay.

Limited Partnerships: Whether it be real estate, gas, or oil, all will fall by at least 50% in the next four years. And you're in one of the most illiquid investments imaginable. Limited partnerships are the second most common reason for investment losses I've observed with clients over the past fifteen years. You might have to take quite a cut in price, assuming you can even extricate yourself. Write it off as an imprudent investment decision of the past. Immediately contact the general partners, and explore the most expeditious ways to dispose of your investment.

Gold/Other Precious Metals: It's important to first consider how close you are to Financial Serenity. If you're "almost home," you might want to keep your gold. If you do, be sure to deduct gold value from the amount available to reach your other investment goals. The story is different for silver and other precious metals. Expect major price declines, and sell. If government debt starts becoming suspect, there might be a time when junk silver coins become very attractive. But would you hold through a price decline in excess of 60%? Even for gold, holding it long-term will likely see some major price declines. This is the risk you take with "buy and hold" strategies. I also favor the use of bullion coins like Maple Leafs over bullion itself, because of better liquidity.

Collectibles: Rare gold coins should not be considered gold, but collectibles. Other coins, stamps, art, and many other items fall into this category. The biggest problem with collectibles is you most likely have an enormous emotional investment in such items. This makes the thought of sale very painful. But that pain should be weighed against the prospect of price declines well in excess of 50%. Does this help ease the pain? This market is also quite thin (not actively traded) when compared to most. If you wait until prices truly start falling, you'll be forced to take large discounts upon sale. The best time to sell anything, particularly these items, is when the market still looks higher and is very liquid.

Savings Bonds: Again, virtually no real return. Safety is superb, however. So these must be viewed as simply a super-safe way to store money. (If you are already at the level of

❖ *Financial Freedom* ❖

Financial Serenity, you can retain them.) You will lose some interest upon early redemption, but go ahead and liquidate if more than six months to maturity.

Your Own Business: It would be naive to suggest selling your current business, particularly if it represents your source of income. Decisions in this area are extremely complex, and your financial wealth in other areas is a critical factor. This book is not designed to provide the simple answers. But business owners or potential chiefs must ponder two critical considerations. First, even the most successful businesses can create serious financial problems when they drain, rather than add to, your capital. If that period occurs, it will most likely be over the next few years. The most important rule: Don't overstay business ownership when you have other options. The next four years will also be the most difficult to start a new business. Because new companies always drain your reserves over the first few years, be very careful.

IRAs: Please don't confuse Individual Retirement Accounts with actual investments. They are only tax-advantaged arrangements, or "boxes," to hold other investments. They make sense if you have enough extra reserves to avoid getting hit with penalties when you might require that money during an emergency. Existing IRAs can be easily transferred into our strategy (unless you bought illiquid partnerships). *Benham or *Scudder will provide transfer papers for you to complete, and they will then directly handle the job of transfer. There are no taxes or penalties for transfer.

Employee Investment Plans: Most larger companies and government employers offer various types of retirement plans. They might be deferred compensation plans or matching investment programs. During "normal" times, they make much sense. But today the dangers might exceed advantages. It depends on how the specific program works, and in partic-

*See Appendix

ular, *the investment options available.* I've conducted tax and investment seminars with CPAs on how to use such programs. But each is different.

As one example, the State of California offers an optional Deferred Compensation Plan and 401K Plan for government workers. Though employees can choose between several types of investments, virtually all are totally inappropriate for the next four years. When last checked, a gold fund was unavailable. Treasury bonds are not an option. Even treasury bills are not available. Money market funds within the program hold no less than 97% commercial paper and CDs. With no way to run, and no place to hide within such a program, the State must gird itself for thousands of angry workers within a short period of time. The declaration of bankruptcy by Orange County was only the tip of the iceberg. Security defaults will move from derivatives to most other investments during the deflation.

More common with larger companies are matching investment programs. The company typically matches 50% of your investment. But that extra 50% doesn't become fully yours to keep until you become "vested," three to five years later. Each year until then the percentage of vesting increases. This sounds like a wonderful deal, and is during normal times. These are not normal times.

To provide a typical example, you invest $1000 this year. The company sets aside $500 in non-vested funds. The following year no vesting occurs. But in the four subsequent years, the company vests $125 a year. In five years you have $1500, right? Not necessarily. It depends on what happens to the price of the underlying investment. With 50% matching, the market would only have to drop 33% to potentially cancel out the extra funds. For stock investments this is entirely likely over the next few years.

Remember two things. First, such optional programs must be classified as illiquid investments, because of the necessity of holding three to five years to fully vest. Second, you have

❖ Financial Freedom ❖

opportunity costs. Your money could be invested in other areas outside the program, and you wouldn't be restricted to which investments you could choose. Given these disadvantages, your choice of investments within the program is critical. Can you move between them? How often? Can you buy safe treasury bills? Long-term treasury bonds? Before using such a program, or deciding to stay in one, you must compare opportunities outside the program to risks inside, whether your funds are tax-advantaged or not. We said long-term treasury bonds and gold stocks offer the greatest potential gains. Are these available in your EIP program? Most likely not.

If your employer's choice of investments does not include a gold fund, a long-term treasury bond fund, or at least the opportunity to buy only treasury bills, it would be very appropriate to make your concerns known immediately. Or to discontinue such plans. Retirement plans at small companies are much more flexible. The company you work for might even consider this investment strategy, including professional management of funds.

As an aside, government and company employers generally contribute regular retirement funds for you. But workers have little influence over how such monies are invested. If your employer screamed loudly during the first phase of the junk bond collapse in 1989, you might express your concern over their questionable investment choices.

4. Starting Your Conventional Account

It is first necessary to determine whether you have more than, or less than, $4000 for investment. We will first assume you have more than this amount. Choose the Mutual Fund Family you will be using. If you closely follow our strategy, the most appropriate would be *Benham.

After deciding, take the following simple steps (we assume the use of *Benham, in order to be as specific as possible):

*See Appendix

- Call *Benham and ask them to send an application (including one or more for any IRAs, either new or transfers from another institution), and a prospectus for their bond, gold, and money market funds.
- After reviewing the prospectus, call them back toll-free and have any and all questions answered. Don't be bashful. Discuss any of your concerns or confusion.
- Complete the application, and mail it with a check addressed to *Benham for at least $1,000, for initial deposit in the money fund, Capital Preservation Fund. This opens your account. You can easily add funds from other sources as other investments are sold. In a few days you will receive confirmation a n d your money fund account number.
- About two weeks after you mail your application you will receive your checkbook.
- The money market (Capital Preservation Fund) is your "base fund." This is the account on which you write checks, and into which you make any and all additional deposits.

If you have less than $4000 in investments, see the discussion under Section Six for starting an investment club. For timely buying and selling, all comments in the following section apply.

5. Conventional Account Investing

From this point on, the actions you take depend on the type of professional assistance you have chosen. If you hire an adviser like *Strayer Investment Advisers, Inc. to buy and sell mutual funds at the most appropriate times, this will be done for you. The adviser will provide regular summaries showing

*See Appendix

how your funds are invested, the totals, and summaries of buys and sells for a nice paper trail at tax time. You will also receive ongoing planning assistance at no extra charge.

If you've subscribed to an adviser's newsletter or Telephone Hotline, you would then be advised by periodic newsletter or start calling the coded hotline to know when to buy or sell the bond, stock, and gold funds. Assuming a 70% bond and 30% gold stock allocation, and $10,000 in your money fund, let's see how this works.

You call and a hotline advises buying bonds. You would then call the toll-free mutual fund phone number and instruct the transfer of about $7,000 from Capital Preservation Fund to the Zero-Coupon Bond Fund of the maturity appropriate for you (usually the year 2010). This transfer takes place at the closing price of the fund at the end of that day. When advised to sell bonds, you again call toll-free and transfer the total back into Capital Preservation Fund. It's that simple.

6. Starting Your Superfund

You can easily start your own group. Share this exciting concept with others, particularly those owning this book. It's not difficult to get several people together.

Remember this is for extremely aggressive investment. For the River City Investment Club in Sacramento, it was determined that no more than 30% be allocated for stock put options, and 70% was earmarked for zero coupon treasury bonds or gold stocks.

So 70% was placed with *Benham. These monies are invested a little differently than they would be if they were in a Conventional Account. One difference is that the club uses the longest-term zero coupon bond fund available—the year 2020. This is a highly-leveraged bond investment, and prices change dramatically as interest rates fluctuate. The gold fund is also quite volatile. The second difference is that the total 70% is invested on a buy signal, whether it be in bonds or

*See Appendix

gold. On occasion, both might be in the buy mode. In this case, that area with the best perceived potential would be emphasized, and receive most, if not all, of this 70% of funds.

You can, of course, also use this basic approach for pooling funds with others for conventional investment. *Strayer Investment Advisers, Inc. is still accepting new investment club accounts for conventional funds (not including options).

7. Superfund Investing

Buying and selling the bond and gold fund portion can be based on an adviser's newsletter or Telephone Hotline, or directly managed by a professional.

The 30% devoted to options is the most difficult to manage. An option can easily move 10% in price in only one day. Therefore, the timing of the purchase and sale, even during a given day, can be critical. Given the fact that perhaps 80% of options buyers lose money, this is a very sophisticated market for professionals only. The potential gain is enormous, but the risks are also extremely high. So you will require professional assistance in this area. You might be able to find a successful local options trader or broker to do this for your club.

8. IRA Investing

Because of their importance, some additional comments on IRAs are appropriate. The procedure for transfer was already described earlier in this chapter.

The attraction of Individual Retirement Accounts is that one does not pay taxes at the end of every year, but only when these monies are withdrawn and used. This means that simple compounding of gains can produce much greater growth than investing with after-tax money, even after taxes are paid on withdrawal. The effect of compounding before-tax money is striking.

For example, assume one's total state and federal taxes are

*See Appendix

❖ Financial Freedom ❖

25%. If you used $2000 in earnings, paid the taxes on that amount, and invested the rest in an account paying 8%, at the end of ten years the account would be worth $2686. This is after deducting taxes on the interest every year.

The same individual, investing the same earnings in an IRA paying the same interest, would after ten years net 20% more ($3238). This is after paying taxes on the total amount, at the end of the period.

If the interest rate were 12%, and after final taxes, the IRA investment would be 31% larger.

In the same scenarios, someone in a 35% total tax bracket would see IRA advantages of 30% and 46% respectively.

The above examples assume the investor would have reached retirement age and be able to withdraw the funds for personal use without IRA early withdrawal penalties. But money grows so much more quickly in an IRA that this vehicle can even be used and money withdrawn before retirement.

If the above individuals were younger and paid a 10% early withdrawal penalty, they would still be ahead by using an IRA. In the 25% tax bracket, and assuming 8% and 12% interest rates, the IRA investments would be worth 4.5% and 13.7% more. In the 35% tax bracket, the IRA investment would show a 10% and 24% advantage. This is after a 10% penalty and after all taxes. So depending on the return on investment and the number of years the funds are invested, don't assume IRAs are only for retirement purposes. Calculate your own numbers to determine whether an IRA is appropriate for you or not. Make sure you confirm IRA early withdrawal penalties, both federal and state, in effect at that time.

One rule of thumb is not to tie up money in an IRA if you haven't set aside emergency funds in a typical, more liquid, investment account. If you and your dependents are not fully insured, including dental, your emergency fund should be larger.

IRAs work well in a Conventional Account. This is because

many mutual funds have much lower minimum investment amounts for IRAs than for regular funds. Most professional investment advisers will manage these funds as well.

One can even place IRA funds in an investment club, and at least 12,000 people in the country are already doing so. It is necessary, however, that a limited partnership be used. Because of this, the approach is not feasible in California. This is because the state for some reason treats limited partnerships in a manner similar to corporations, and imposes a minimum tax even on such investment clubs. This tax increased an astounding 300% over a five year period, and in 1995 is $800 a year. It is hoped that California will join most other state and federal regulators in recognizing the importance of increasing savings and investment, and eventually exempt investment club limited partnerships from this tax. It is necessary to confirm how limited partnerships are handled in your state.

9. New Found Money

The final step is to start carving Found Money out of your expenses, and moving it into your conventional or aggressive account. Every time you make a deposit with *Benham or *Scudder, you receive a confirmation and a new deposit slip and envelope. And it's a good habit to make a contribution every month into your investment club. Found Money that isn't invested regularly tends to get spent.

You're now on your way. In its simplest form, all you have to do is determine how much to place into a regular investment account or very aggressive fund. Whether your net financial worth is $25, $25 thousand, or more. The four-year reward is never having to concern yourself with earning money again.

*See Appendix

10

Vigilance and More Growth

> *The battle, sir, is not to the strong alone;*
> *it is to the vigilant, the active, the brave.*
> —Patrick Henry

YOUR NEW STRATEGY is now in place and working. You know where you're headed, why, and how to get there. You now have a receptacle for regular investment funds and very aggressive funds.

You will now start to sense a new freedom. Your confidence about money grows. You know you're not investing in things you don't understand, and the safety of your investments is much greater. Your new investments are also very liquid. You can get to them and access your money immediately whenever you want or need to. Your financial situation is also greatly simplified. You no longer have dribs and drabs of money all over the place. Your money is always working for you. You no longer have much in checking accounts that don't pay any interest. Financial fears are greatly reduced.

But some vigilance is still required. You will still be extremely tempted to jump at those sweet deals a broker or friend point out. Just say no; they don't fit your strategy.

Vigilance is even more important for your Found Money.

It's necessary to keep putting it aside and moving it into your two investment areas. For cash, put it into a can or piggy bank. For your checking account or credit cards, think twice before buying something that's not planned. At the end of every month, empty your growing cash store into your checking account. Then "sweep" those extra reserves into the money fund of your new account with a single monthly check.

Continue to beware of new debt. A friend, Mike Duckworth, uses the term G.O.D.—Get Out of Debt. The key now is S.O.D.—Stay Out of Debt. In the Lord's Prayer, the phrase "and forgive us our debts, as we forget our debtors," now becomes more meaningful. Any expectation creates a debt, and demands that we or someone else do something. Monetary debt requires us or someone else to repay something. Shakespeare was certainly clear when he said "Never a lender nor a borrower be." If everyone had followed those important words, we would never have inflation or deflation. But does this mean we should never lend someone money? Basically, yes. Doing so might enable the individual to avoid taking responsibility for change, and getting his financial house in order. Charity—giving without imposing expectations—is the new alternative.

But we're not finished yet. There are even more opportunities for getting our financial house in order. We've already acted on reducing expenses. But that's only half the equation. We naturally want to minimize outgo, but anyone can also increase income. This is our final focus.

Increasing Income (For Employees)

Let's first discuss some opportunities for those who work for someone else. What follows has always been available to us. But we simply never before had the motivation to do it. Now we fully realize our specific goals and dreams are at stake. And if we act to increase income immediately, more funds will be available for the investment opportunities of the next few years. In other words, if we can fully load our two

❖ *Vigilance and More Growth* ❖

investment areas now, before the fireworks start, we can be home after 1998.

We've already discussed accessing cash value of life insurance policies. But because so many people can take advantage of this opportunity, it should be repeated. The majority of Americans have no savings or investments except for insurance cash value, perhaps retirement funds where they work, and existing home equity. Don't overlook this method of obtaining additional investment funds.

If you're a commissioned salesman, now is the time to buckle under and pull out all the stops. If you operate from a sales floor, offer to take others' shifts to be available for additional sales. This is the equivalent of working overtime. Now is the time to do it. Increase your education by learning more about the product and learning more effective selling techniques. Join clubs and organizations to increase your contact with potential buyers. Make a point to ask others what they do. This provides the opportunity to tell them what you do, and to keep you in mind when they might need your product or service.

If you're paid by the hour, work some overtime. Even if you're salaried, this will increase the amount of work you do, making you more valuable to the company.

You might want to change jobs. There can be advantages and disadvantages to this. If you have several years' seniority, you might be one of the last to get laid off as economic conditions tighten. Never underestimate the value of seniority. Also be careful not to move out of one industry that will perform better during economic difficulties, only to hire on at a company that will not do as well. How truly important are the company's products or services to the average person? Most importantly, never leave one job until you have another. I'm amazed at how many people get angry with their current employer or overestimate their own market value, and simply walk. No one should allow his company to walk all over him, but swallow your pride and anger until you line up something else.

Take a part-time job to increase income. If ever in your life you might do this, now is the time. Two jobs now, before the deflation, are worth several times that in four years. We've all heard our parents and grandparents talk about doing this. Anyone could do so if they really wanted to. And if it's doing something we would enjoy, we might even experience more personal satisfaction from the second job. Having more diverse work experiences would also make us more marketable in the future for a new position. And it's proof to a potential employer of our willingness to work.

Be vigilant of management-labor problems with local businesses. If you're working at very low wages now, or are free to take a new job, this will offer tremendous opportunities. As a deflation sets in, companies will try to negotiate lower wages with employees just to stay alive. Some labor groups won't understand the importance of flexible wages, won't know what's happening, and feel they're being cheated. They will strike. In many cases the company will simply hire new workers. Be vigilant and ready to act quickly in such situations. Union workers must also take heed of such developments. Be extremely careful about supporting votes to increase or maintain wages beyond reason. The result could be the total loss of a job.

Start a part-time business. Now is the time to review Chapter Four, when you defined your time resources and talents. By listing all the things you know more about, or can do better than most people, you identified potential activities. Or perhaps you simply have a lot of time available. One word of warning: Think twice about whether or not it will require significant start-up money. Keep expenses ridiculously low, and even work out of your home if possible. The latter, in fact, will actually attract several customers, because they would know you can charge lower prices because of low overhead. Remember, you're trying to increase income, not increase outgo or pride.

By being creative and looking for opportunities, you'll determine other ways to use your extra time, talents, and re-

❖ *Vigilance and More Growth* ❖

sources. And don't forget trade and barter.

But the most practical way for most people to increase income is by becoming more valuable to their employers. A better attitude alone will increase the likelihood of larger-than-normal raises (or prevent being among the first to be laid off). First, simply make up your mind whether you're going to stay with a company or work elsewhere. If you're going to continue where you are, you'd better make the best of it. If you can't do something about a problem you encounter, let it go. If you can see a better way, share your idea. The biggest pet peeve of business managers is employees who complain about things but don't have a better way.

You can also become more valuable by learning new skills. Determine what the company provides in training to pursue additional abilities. But even if you take a few courses on your own (and be sure to share such actions with your supervisor) the rewards can be higher-paying positions or salary increases. In this computer age, learning how to use a computer might be a logical first step.

But even these ideas might fail if there is no communication between employee and company. Any employee has the right to know how he's doing, and where he might be going in the company, preferably through a management review. Ask for one. If your small company doesn't have a management review process, force one. If you don't, you run the substantial risk of looking for a new job later, and having no written proof of how you were regarded at your previous job.

If your company doesn't have such a procedure, ask your manager for a written review. Tell him you will provide the form. If the response is not positive, offer to buy lunch and do it then. Make a copy of the following review form, which I've used in management consulting work with small companies. It was adapted from one of the best-managed corporations in the country, Caterpillar, Inc. If you're a manager, why not use it to set up a review program?

First, the manager and employee complete the form in advance, independently. The two then meet and compare notes, and agree on a compromise rating for each area and for the total. There are also five questions. Discuss each, and after assuring both agree on the position's job priorities, arrive at a joint understanding of:

- The employee's major assets
- What the employee could do to perform the job even better
- What the manager or others will do to assist better performance
- Future job opportunities or plans for the employee

The cooperative manager will agree to briefly summarize these points in writing for the employee.

MANAGEMENT REVIEW

Point Range

MANAGEMENT/WORK STYLE

Aware of highest priorities; sets challenging personal goals; achieves results; works by project; completes assignments on time and follows up; plans for action; makes decisions; plans for future; results and profit-oriented; has initiative and drive.   40 —— 0

TEAMWORK

Helps others naturally without interfering; keeps company/group goals in balance with own; conscious and supportive of time, efforts, and goals of others; draws out and supports the best in others; helps build positive reputations for co-workers.   20 —— 0

❖ *Vigilance and More Growth* ❖

LEADERSHIP

    Contributes to an efficient company; shares expertise with associates; creates interest; commands respect; has desire to be outstanding; accepts responsibility; has concern for the future; has frustration tolerance; has self-confidence.   20 —— 0

COMMUNICATIONS AND RELATIONS

    Communications are factual, timely, and concise. Keeps others informed of major activities; keeps good files; good oral expressions. Maintains good client and peer relations; is fair and trustworthy.   10 —— 0

COST CONTROL AND CASH FLOW

    Obtains value for cost; operates within budget; shares ideas on cost savings. Aware of seasonal declines in cash flow and immediately and spontaneously responds in assisting the situation.   10 —— 0

                                   TOTAL   100 —— 0

1. STRENGTHS Briefly describe the major assets you believe are of influence in the current job.

2. IMPROVEMENT OPPORTUNITIES Describe any job-related abilities which could be further developed to enable achievement of even better performance.

3. ASSISTANCE REQUESTED What things could others provide, in the way of assistance or tools, to help performance at this position?

4. PERSONAL/JOB RELATED Describe personal plans to achieve objectives related to the present job. These are related to the job but are personal objectives which are primarily within the employee's control.

5. ASPIRATIONS Briefly describe future job interests that are within one's ability but are challenging.

Increasing Income (For the Self-Employed)

If you own your own business, there are even more ways to increase income. Let's discuss some of the most important. The most obvious is to increase sales. But it's difficult to gain a fresh perspective from the inside. Consider bringing in a professional who can provide a new, clear perspective. But because recommendations can involve much additional time or money on your part, think about this: Enter into an agreement with the consultant by which he is compensated based on a percentage of the net incremental profits he or his ideas generate.

Provide additional products or services. Some can be natural extensions of your business. The above professional could provide some insight. Just make sure that incremental profits exceed additional costs.

Employ salespeople paid strictly on commission. Also consider a profit-sharing plan with current employees as an added incentive for them to increase business. Current employees are the most obvious and effective "salespeople."

If necessary, trade out your current business or personal expenses for the products or services you provide. Your additional "income" is equal to the profit margin on what you provide. For maximum benefit: Always barter expenses you're paying cash for today and with people whose business you're not getting today.

❖ *Vigilance and More Growth* ❖

There are numerous ways to cut costs, but we often don't take the time to search them out. By offering incentives to employees to find them, more will be identified.

Employee costs can be reduced by making more employees subcontractors. There are strict federal limitations on this practice, but if feasible you can reduce FICA and other wage-related costs. Be sure to consult your CPA for assistance.

Sell or rent your extra resources. Plant, equipment, and office space can usually be more heavily burdened. Why not rent it out during those times it's not being used?

Restructure debt. Consolidation can work for businesses as well as individuals. You can also negotiate lower payments with creditors. Consider the benefits of selling company equity either to repay current debt or as an alternative to acquiring new debt.

Duplicate yourself with new outlets or by franchising. But instead of incurring the costs of expansion, focus on the receiving of rights or a percentage of profits from others who would benefit from identifying with your firm or its practices.

Consider hiring your older kids, with their lower tax rate, as a less-expensive way to channel funds into your family. Consult your tax professional.

It might be a blow to your ego, and in particular to your efforts to control, but there is another important option. This is to take another job, and replace yourself with a less-expensive employee.

Vigilance of Your New Strategy

Some will find it more difficult than others to break old belief systems about money, and change old, inappropriate investment habits. So we must be very careful not to repeat certain patterns. This might be a good time to summarize the most important do's and don'ts alluded to earlier.

Don't be paranoid about taxes. This is the single, most common, cause of major investment losses. People try so hard to avoid paying taxes that they often end up creating financial disasters. The most common development is buying a home to "write off interest payments on income taxes." As real estate plummets in price, this error will become rudely apparent.

Tax paranoia created the greatest investment loss I've ever seen. Several years ago a client sold a huge interest in a successful company. He asked us to manage a very sizable sum. In two years the entire amount was gone. Not because we weren't making it grow, because we were. There was another problem. His CPA, in order to sharply reduce his taxes, talked him into buying a tax-advantaged land deal. As rental income on the property fell and his payments remained the same, his investment became a virtual alligator, eating up hundreds of thousands of dollars. That client forgot that any tax-advantaged investment must also make total economic sense.

Along the same vein, I see mounting problems in employee investment programs and deferred compensation plans where people work. If someone is in the 35% tax bracket, this might seem like a "savings" of 35% or more. Remember, this is not your money. It's a "government loan." Only if the investment grows and compounds is this an advantage. The problem is that most of these plans do not provide adequate investment choices for the next four years. Does your program allow you to buy treasury bonds, gold stock funds, or at least treasury bills? Most do not. Instead, the choices are normally limited to stock funds, various insurance company products, corporate bond funds, and (if a corporation) stock in that company. Billions will be lost in these investments over the next four years, more than wiping out any perceived tax advantages.

Another rule is to never buy limited partnerships that do not allow you to sell your interests without penalties or long delays. This is the second most common reason for investment losses that I've observed. There are also increasing numbers of these partnerships that once provided liquidity but have frozen investors' funds because of growing financial problems.

Next, save to invest. Particularly if you have no investment funds now, seed money is required to take advantage of the

❖ *Vigilance and More Growth* ❖

opportunities available. We have already discussed numerous ways to develop Found Money. But the bottom line is that if you have nothing to invest, nothing will be gained. And now is the time to get started.

Venture forward. Many are today investing in what they consider "safe" investments. The concept of safety will change dramatically within a short period of time. And we have already discussed the marginal real return on several investments, once taxes and inflation are removed. If you are close to financial serenity, holding treasury bonds and physical gold makes a lot of sense. Otherwise, playing it safe and collecting simple interest on most investments will eventually lead to not only little to no return, but the growing possibility of losing your investment principal.

Don't buy and hold. All investments go up and down in value. Some fluctuate in value over a period of some seven years, and others over decades. But nothing is a long-term buy and hold. It makes total common sense to periodically buy and sell any investment. Only in this way can real return be maximized.

Assure potential reward exceeds risk. Again, real risk is much higher than is apparent with most investments over the next four years. And real reward is much less than it appears after taxes and inflation.

Be consistent and patient. Now that you have a sound investment strategy, evaluate its effectiveness over a period of years. Allowing emotions to intervene or introducing a mixture of different approaches will only confuse. Patience will be rewarded.

Keep it simple. Chasing too many strategies or different types of investments simply allows you to know less and less about more and more. By keeping things simple your life will not only experience less confusion, but time will be saved. This action also allows you to focus upon and become more familiar with those few areas that make the most sense.

Finally, don't assume more risk than is necessary. As you approach financial serenity or retirement, avoid investments or approaches with greater risk of loss than necessary. If you are young or have a lot of financial ground to make up, greater risks can be assumed to use this unique period to reach your goals.

We have already warned against using this strategy with a current mutual fund family. With rapid changes in mutual fund offerings we cannot assure that *Benham and *Scudder are the only families that meet all of our strategy requirements. The most important criteria should nevertheless be that they offer a government money market fund, that preferably only holds treasury bills. The reason, again, is that regular money funds might be frozen when you want to take advantage of a soaring treasury bond or gold fund. Such a flight to safety could happen overnight, as it did in October, 1987. Flight would be out of commercial paper and CDs that comprise most money funds, and into treasurys and gold investments.

Very early we said that it is not possible to mix this strategy with one you might be using now. Use one or the other, but don't try to mix the two. If tempted, the following explains how to approach this.

Let's assume you believe that 50/60 year cycles, 7-year cycles, and our investment indicators for determining when to buy and sell are hogwash. In other words, deflation and timing strategies don't make sense. Instead of rejecting such a scenario and strategy, determine what percentage of your net worth you would bet against such developments. Keep that percentage in real estate, stocks, CDs, or anything else you're now using. Place the remainder into this strategy. Then, every few months, re-evaluate your decision. As a deflation becomes more obvious, the debt problem grows, more corporations and financial institutions declare bankruptcy, and the value and safety of your other investments fall, move more money into this strategy.

In summary, the strategy we have developed is as effective as virtually any being currently employed by others. It is simple, includes specific objectives, is time-based, and includes a

*See Appendix

❖ *Vigilance and More Growth* ❖

clear and concise action plan. But never forget what you are trying to accomplish.

Over the next four years your goal is to decrease, and finally eliminate, your debt-to-capital ratio. This can be done by eliminating debt, and you now understand the urgent reasons for doing so. You can also accomplish this goal by greatly increasing your capital, i.e., the total size and purchasing power of your investments.

It's obvious we want to grow from what might be a very limited initial amount of savings or investment, by using those investments with the best growth potential. We won't get there by basically storing our money in areas that provide little to no return after taxes and inflation. Your new strategy provides for this.

During the dangerous and volatile period we are now entering, it's impossible to anticipate all economic and financial developments over the next several years. This makes it imperative we not buy illiquid investments. There is no way to know when we might need to quickly move funds into a different area. Your new strategy allows for this.

Simply increasing our wealth means nothing if we do not maintain safe investments. We have chosen only the safest for our strategy. Again, given the horrendous levels of debt in this country, we must be prepared for unbelievable developments in future years. We've already indicated that even the safety of government debt, as represented by treasury bonds and treasury bills, might eventually become questionable. It's impossible to anticipate when alternative stores of value might be necessary and appropriate. We can only be vigilant and try to stay ahead of such developments.

And never, ever, forget one thing. Wealth is increased or maintained not only by participating in those markets that rise, but also by *avoiding falling markets*. Your new strategy also provides for this critical consideration.

11

Financial Seeking

*Education is...hanging around
until you've caught on.*
                —Robert Frost

WE'VE COME A long way. Our financial understanding and its application have grown by leaps and bounds. From here on growth will be slower, but more relaxed and confident. We've reached the phase called refinement.

Our investment universe has been greatly reduced and simplified. This makes it possible to become extremely knowledgeable about those few areas that are so critical and offer the most potential over the next few years.

Although strictly optional, we'll now share some of the most appropriate ways to put a finishing touch on your new financial and economic prowess.

Reread Chapter Two as many times as necessary until you totally absorb the meaning and the causes of inflation and deflation. Also use the inflation formula in several personal examples until you get used to adjusting investments (and "prices") for taxes and inflation. Update the Consumer Price Index often to keep your CPI chart up to date. Your library can provide the most recent CPI.

Reread Chapter Six, the section on treasury bonds, as often as necessary until you fully absorb how bond prices change. Really internalize how and why bond prices move inversely to interest rates and why interest rates change.

Read a book about gold. Learn about the role it has always played as money, why governments hate it, how its price changes, and more. If you have difficulty finding such books your local library can assist, even by ordering a loaner book from other libraries.

Read a book about contrary opinion as it relates to investing. You will never again make the mistake of "following the crowd." Again, your library can assist.

Read a book about stock options and index options. Or at least contact a stockbroker and ask for their free brochure on stock options. In particular, learn how put options work.

The Wall Street Journal is one of the best newspapers in the world. If you can afford it, I suggest you subscribe for at least three months. Call to determine details, and perhaps they will provide a special introductory offer. If you can't afford it, arrange to regularly receive someone else's after he's done with it, or frequent your library for a period. The following tips will speed your learning from this excellent information source:

It's not necessary to read the entire paper. It provides much more detail than you'll need. Quickly check the summary in the second column, front page. Read referred articles about banks, savings and loans (and credit unions), and any special articles on economic trends (often in column five, page one). Always read the editorial page, to stay on top of major developments. For any article, however, always question the vested interest of anyone quoted or writing the report. Get in the habit of checking for this first, before reading any article.

Read every day the Foreign Exchange and particularly the Credit Markets sections (see page one Contents for page numbers). Some items will be a little confusing at first, but over time you'll quickly learn how new debt, debt quality, trade balances, currency changes, economic activity, and interest rates (U.S. and foreign) influence one another (watch for patterns). You'll also start to notice that future projections by in-

*See Appendix

❖ *Financial Seeking* ❖

dividuals are usually wrong (again, watch for vested interests of quoted individuals).

Also read every day the Precious Metals commentary in the Commodities section. Again, watch for patterns (and quotes by vested interests). It's not necessary to read the stock market detail. Everyone has an opinion, most have vested interests, and the majority is generally wrong. Articles on page C1, however, often give clues to new trends, sane or insane.

You will tend to pick it up mostly from articles about the banking system and the Credit Markets section, but as the deflation unfolds, watch for these developments, in approximately the following order: Problems with derivatives, further collapse in the junk bond market (as interest rates rise to reflect growing risk), downgrading and lower prices of higher-quality corporate bonds, collapsing financial institutions (more problems with their junk bonds, overseas loans, and real estate), increasing problems for Uncle Sam in bailing out financial institutions, problems and defaults with municipal bonds, growing corporate bankruptcies, lowering of guarantees on bank/S&L deposits, federal problems in disposing of failed S&L and bank assets... and further down the road, risk questions of owning long-term treasury bonds (as deficits soar and the debt gets bigger and bigger), and finally worries about treasury bills themselves.

"The Journal" also has several fun articles. Keep an eye on the fourth column of page one, and the lower left article on page B1.

Regardless of your sources, you will even be able to eventually sense economic change from social developments. When the economy is topping out you will hear and see bizarre and perhaps even disgusting social trends. This would include dance crazes very sexual in nature, songs that are revolting in their verbiage, daring fashion trends, ignored environmental issues, press about satanic/demonic rituals, violence and horror themes on TV and in movies, concentration on growing health problems, poor divorce statistics, wars and international discord, etc.

On the other hand, healthier economic times go hand in hand with more conservative dance themes, more loving popular songs (including new age music and the classics), more conservative fashion trends, increased concern for the earth and our animal friends, increasing spirituality, growing androgynous trends, more loving and humorous TV and movie themes, positive health developments, families coming together and staying together, worldwide cooperation and peaceful developments, etc.

When these trends start to manifest it can be easy to spot shifts in the 50/60 year cycle. But if you become sufficiently aware, subtle changes can even alert you to changes in 7-year cycles.

In order to learn of future trends we must still be vigilant of our sources of information. Anyone or any source projecting future developments must be scrutinized for conflict of interest or bias. Also be aware that those unaware of these major cycles will tend to project the future based on projection of trends of the last few decades. Every 50-60 years all trends reverse violently. Once you understand this you can fully benefit from those changes, and better assist those who don't.

As stated, these pursuits are strictly optional. But at least you now know what to look for, and where, if you choose to further sharpen your investment acumen.

12

Financial Sharing

*I am indeed rich,
since my income is superior to my expense,
and my expense is equal to my wishes.*
—Gibbon

THERE ARE TWO ways we can share financially. The first is by sharing our new concept of money and debt with others. There are several ways to do this. As most people don't even understand inflation, and that it has taken an entire book to explain sensible investment, any of your brief explanations will fall on deaf or unknowing ears. So the best way is to share this book with parents, friends, and even your children. All will learn the danger of debt. The only question is whether it will be learned by advance education or painful experience.

Our first choices will probably be our immediate family, who will influence our future wealth. If our parents can learn about how to deal with debt and investment through a copy of this book, more funds will be available via inheritance and family legacy.

If each of our children learns these precepts, they will enter the adult world with better tools for understanding. By learning about debt, budgeting, saving, and investing from an early age, numerous financial problems and worries will be avoided. With a firm financial footing, they will more quickly stand on their own and help others, instead of depending on you for financial help. Or, horrors, have to move back home!

If your friends learn what's happening and why, and early enough, you will eventually receive their gratitude for pointing out the problems and opportunities. A copy of this book might be the only avenue for doing this. Trying to "convince" them yourself won't work. Without the full story, they won't be able to understand.

The greatest potential for overall change, of course, is at the hands of our elected officials. Now that you understand how our system really works, do you want your voice to be heard for creating a new, fresh order in the future of your city, your state, or your country? Write or call your mayor, state representative, and congressional representatives and senators, expressing your new views.

Tell them about your deep concerns about new debt, questionable expenditures, and the proliferation of new laws that only try to patch old errors. Pass along your desires that major decisions be returned to local levels. Particularly for our friends in Washington, express your concern about the destruction of our currency by government-induced inflation, the need for securing our currency by the return of at least a partial gold standard, the hopeless support of major industries and financial institutions while individuals are lost to the system, and the need to stop the terrifying escalation of federal debt.

The tone of your communication is important. If you accuse or attack, fully expect a defense or rationalization as a response. Simply express your deep concern about such developments. But don't be afraid to write a second letter if you receive a "boiler plate" response. Tell them you were disappointed by the generalities in their reply and that you are seriously concerned. Incidentally, if you don't know the names and addresses of your elected representatives, call your mayor's office, the library, or the post office.

The second way we can share financially is with money

❖ *Financial Sharing* ❖

itself. But again, real charity does not involve expectations. That only creates more problems. As a rule we don't do this very well. *The Bible* even describes the difficulty when it says it's more difficult for a camel to pass through the eye of a needle than for a rich man to find heaven. This simply describes the enormous responsibility of wealth. We are all equal. But if one is "richer," this automatically implies inequality. Wealth is, therefore, meant to be shared.

I've wrestled with this problem for years and have developed an answer for myself. I've decided that aside from typical charity, anything in excess of financial serenity be divided in thirds. One-third must be spent on myself. I can't save it but it must be spent, and not on things I'd planned (which would create expectations). One-third must be given to others, anonymously when possible. The final third must be invested to produce even more for the other two entities. I believe it difficult for the universe to deny the success of this.

The giving of money can be extremely difficult to do without expectations. We generally fail. Until we better understand the ramifications, anonymous giving is the most appropriate, with the recipient knowing nothing of our identity. Have you ever given something to or done something for someone without identifying yourself? Or without even telling others what you've done? The effect is absolutely exhilarating. This is the payoff for giving out of no motivation other than true charity and gratitude.

The best way to teach is still by example. Because what we teach, that is, what we do, we are learning. We still have the most control over our own finances. And by getting out of debt and getting our own houses in order, we become part of the solution and better able to help those in need.

It should now be clearly obvious that money is not the root of all evil. It is instead our relationship to money that's the problem. Is it a dysfunctional relationship and do we have an unhealthy investment in it? Do we suffer from a perceived lack that prevents us from full realization, or are we enmeshed in greed? Or do we come from abundance and generosity regardless of our financial worth?

For many people the problem lies with the expenditure side instead of the income side. And these are after-tax dollars! We can certainly learn humility and become appropriate with our living standards. When we remove debt we're not only simplifying our lives but removing a terrible burden.

For others the problem is with greed. Perhaps we're mired in both lack and greed. Few people escape from greed of some kind. But what you do about it is certainly your choice. In the end, any relationship provides the basis for misguided grandiosity or wonderful grandeur. This includes money.

Sometimes we learn the most from those younger, those with a clearer, less-confused perspective. I learned much about wealth from one particular teenager. In 1987 I taught a twelve-week study course called "The Masters Program." That course concentrated on investing and the psychology of money. The supposed purpose of one homework assignment was to help the students identify specific financial objectives. Each had the option of remaining anonymous if he wished, and we discussed individual written responses as a group. I asked each to identify how he would spend three increasing amounts of money. To specify an end point in their financial quest and avoid greed, the final question was "At what point would you consider yourself wealthy?" Our youngest group member, our teenager, had written "Wealth is a state of mind. I am wealthy today." David has now completed his study in Philosophy and Religion. That night, however, we were his pupils.

In conclusion, I hope you now have a much healthier attitude about wealth. What you once considered massive economic problems, personal financial worries, or simply concerns about how to best invest, should now be seen in terms of opportunities.

Knowledge eliminates fear. And my primary objective has been to immediately steer you on a secure course that you understand and which offers financial serenity. Yet as you near

❖ *Financial Sharing* ❖

your destination, you will certainly arrive at one important conclusion: Money and possessions are not the most important things in life. But financial fears can certainly obscure the path to happiness. If my objective has been accomplished, your financial fears will dissolve.

In the end you will likely have one of three reactions to what was presented. You might declare this book interesting, and then lay it aside, doing nothing. This is the fate of most books. In such a case, I have failed to convince you that you deserve abundance, or that such a strategy applies to you.

Or you might consider those developments described as possible, but will take a "wait and see" attitude. The longer you delay, the lesser the opportunities available.

Or you will immediately act to get your financial house in order and obtain the ongoing assistance to maximize your finances. Knowing you have done everything professionally possible investment-wise, you will then truly start to live. As the described changes fall into place, you will finally conclude there truly is a Higher Order at work. As you are finally free to concentrate on self-development and spiritual growth, everyone will benefit from your newly-found abundance. During this new period of unfathomable change, you will be part of the glorious solution, not part of the problem.

The choice is yours.

Glossary of Terms

Apollo Strategy—A proprietary strategy used by Strayer Investment Advisers, Inc., that matches one's financial reserves (or lack of) with specific achievable financial goals (including Financial Serenity, Financial Security, Debt-Free, and Shelter Secure).

Annuity—An investment contract sold by life insurance companies that specifies a fixed or variable payment to be paid to the annuitant at some future time.

Call Option—A financial contract, purchased at market price, granting the option owner the right to *buy* a specific security at a particular price within a specified time period. Most options are rarely exercised, but instead are bought and sold before expiration, in an effort to benefit from the rise and fall in options prices. Call option buyers expect the security in question to rise in price.

Certificate of Deposit (CD)—A debt instrument issued by a bank, ranging in maturity from less than one year to several years. At the bank's discretion, they may allow you to withdraw your funds before maturity, in which case 2-3 months of interest is forfeited.

COLAG—A market indicator calculated by dividing the index of coincident indicators by the index of lagging indicators, both of which are published monthly by the federal government.

Commercial Paper—Short term, unsecured, obligations issued by banks, corporations, and other borrowers, with maturities ranging from 2 to 270 days.

Commodity Futures—(see Futures Contracts)

Consumer Price Index (CPI)—A measure of changes in consumer prices, as determined by a monthly survey of the U.S. Bureau of Labor Statistics.

Conventional Account—A method for achieving investment goals, that employs conventional investment techniques and investments offering the least likelihood of major loss, while maintaining above average safety, liquidity, and growth potential.

Corporate Bond—A long-term debt instrument issued by a private corporation. Corporate bondholders have precedence over shareholders for any claims on company assets upon bankruptcy, because bondholders are creditors.

Cycle, 7-Year—A recurring period of 6-10 years (averaging 7 years in length), that defines the periodicity of recessions.

Cycle, 54-Year—A recurring period of 50-60 years (averaging 54 years in length), that defines the periodicity of major deflations/depressions.

Deflation Cycle—A recurring period of 50-60 years (averaging 54 years in length), that defines the periodicity of major deflations/depressions.

❖ *Glossary of Terms* ❖

Deflation, Monetary—A significant decrease in the supply of money, usually caused by defaults on previously incurred levels of debt.

Deflation, Price—An increase in the domestic purchasing power of a currency. This appears, however, as a decrease in general price levels, including consumer goods, wages and certain markets.

Depression—A severe, and generally lengthy, reduction in economic activity, typically accompanied by failures of financial institutions, falling prices (deflation), and a sharp reduction in the money supply. Depressions generally occur every 50-60 years (see Cycles, 54-Year), and serve to sharply reduce or even eliminate debt incurred over several prior decades.

Derivatives—Financial contacts whose value is "derived" from reference to some underlying financial instrument or index. The most recognized derivatives are futures contracts and options, but countless other more esoteric instruments have been securitized. When used to "hedge" against price movements in other securities they can play an important financial role. More recently, however, they have earned a negative reputation because of outright heavily-leveraged speculations on anticipated market developments, often resulting in huge losses and even the bankruptcy of institutions incorrectly using such instruments.

Discount Rate—The interest rate the Federal Reserve System charges banks for loans from the federal government.

Elliott Wave Theory—A detailed description of how markets behave in predictable recurring waves, for the purpose of predicting market price/time events. Emphasis is on how mass investor psychology swings from pessimism to optimism and back in a natural sequence, creating specific patterns in price movement. Robert Prechter is the current leading figure in Elliott Wave Principle.

Federal Funds Rate—The interest rate at which banks lend federal funds to each other on an overnight basis. Federal funds are monies deposited by commercial banks at Federal Reserve Banks, including funds in excess of bank reserve requirements.

Federal Reserve Board (FRB)—The governing board of the Federal Reserve System. Comprised of seven individuals appointed by the President, subject to Senate confirmation, who serve 14-year terms. Purpose is to protect the purchasing power of the dollar, but the FRB periodically chooses to influence business conditions. The Board establishes policies such as reserve requirements and other bank regulations, sets the discount rate, tightens or loosens the availability of credit in the economy, and regulates the purchase of securities on margin.

Free Reserves—The amount of excess reserves in the banking system above minimum reserve requirements.

Futures Contract—The agreement to buy or sell a specific amount of a commodity or financial instrument at a particular price in a stipulated future month. Leveraging is typically very large, and only a small fraction of the total value of the contract is required in advance (with the remainder borrowed from the broker). If prices move sufficiently against the investor, additional margins are typically required. Due to enormous leveraging, profits and losses can be well in excess of the initial investment.

Gold Standard—A monetary system under which units of circulated currency are convertible into gold. At this time no country in the world is currently under the gold standard. (Without a gold standard, few countries can resist inflating their money supply and financial developments tend to become very chaotic.)

❖ *Glossary of Terms* ❖

Government Agency Bond—Long-term debt obligations of one of several federal agencies. These are indirect obligations of the federal government, while treasury bills, notes, and bonds are direct obligations.

Hyperinflation—Very high levels of inflation, that often results in the total destruction of the currency in question, and ending in depression.

Individual Retirement Accounts (IRA)—A personal, tax deferred, retirement account for use by an employed individual. Instead of an investment per se, these are arrangements into which one can place most other investments. Company retirement funds can usually be transferred into an IRA when the employee leaves the company, and IRAs can be transferred from one institution to another, both without penalty. The two greatest advantages are one has complete control over the types of securities used, and gains compound until funds are withdrawn. Withdrawals prior to age 59½ are generally subject to a 10% (of principal) penalty tax.

Indicator—A specific series of financially-based data that correlates closely with future prices of common stocks, bonds, or gold stocks. Indicators are weighed and combined to create the Sentinel Index.

Inflation, Monetary—A significant increase in the supply of money, usually caused by an increase in debt.

Inflation, Price—A decrease in the domestic purchasing power of currency. This appears, however, as an increase in general price levels, including consumer goods, wages and certain markets.

Junk Bonds—Corporate bonds issued by companies without long track records of sales and earnings, or by those with questionable credit strength (rated BB or lower by rating agencies).

Kondratieff Wave—A phenomenon first identified by Nikolai Kondratieff in the 1920s, that identifies cycles of economic growth and collapse in capitalistic counties. Synonymous with the 54-year cycle. In brief, every 50-60 years (averaging 54 years) debt increases to levels that can no longer be serviced; debt defaults, bankruptcy, and economic decline force elimination of most debt; and then the process starts all over again. Interestingly, social and health cycles follow the same periodicity.

Liquidity—The speed and ease by which one can buy or sell an investment at fair market price. One of three critical requirements for any investment during periods of massive economic and financial change.

Load Mutual Fund—An investment company that receives monies from large numbers of shareholders and invests such funds in specific types of securities (as defined in the prospectus of that particular fund). Contrary to no-load funds, purchase commissions are charged, that are generally paid to the salesman or broker promoting the product.

Minimum Reserve Requirement—A percentage (currently about 10%) of any deposit that a bank must place in reserves. This number is established by the Federal Reserve Board.

Money Market Fund—A special type of no-load mutual fund that only invests in short-term securities. Liquidity is excellent and most such funds even provide a checkbook for easy withdrawals. Some money market funds only invest in government securities and others invest in myriad short-term instruments.

Municipal Bond—A long-term debt instrument issued by a state or local government. Are generally exempt from federal taxes and under certain conditions from state and local taxes.

❖ *Glossary of Terms* ❖

Mutual Fund—(see No-Load Mutual Fund and Load Mutual Fund)

Net Asset Value—The market value of a mutual fund share, synonymous with bid price. For no-load funds, the NAV, market price, and offering price are the same. For load funds, prices are quoted after adding sales charges to the net asset value.

No-Load Mutual Fund—An investment company that receives monies from large numbers of shareholders and invests such funds in specific types of securities (as defined in the prospectus of that particular fund). No-load funds do not charge a purchase commission, generally paid to the salesman or broker promoting the product. This is a popular method for investing in a given type of market, for increased liquidity, diversification, and simplicity.

Options—(see Put Option or Call Option)

Put Option—A financial contract, purchased at market price, granting the option owner the right to sell a specific security at a particular price within a specified time period. Most options are rarely exercised, but instead are bought and sold before expiration, in an effort to benefit from the rise and fall in options prices. This is one of the few practical ways an investor can profit from declining securities prices.

Real Estate Investment Trust (REIT)—Typically, a publicly traded company that manages a portfolio of real estate in order to earn profits for shareholders. REITs are very similar to mutual funds, except for their focus on real estate, which involves different regulations from stock and bond investments.

Real Growth Potential—The degree of monetary return possible, after tax and after inflation. Return must also sufficiently compensate for risk. One of three critical requirements for any investment during periods of massive economic and financial change.

Recession—A short-lived downturn in economic activity, typically measured by two or more consecutive quarters of decline in Gross Domestic Product. Recessions are usually accompanied by increases in inventories and an increase in interest rates (often pushed higher by the Federal Reserve Board to combat rising inflation or attract investment funds from abroad). Recessions generally occur every 6-10 years (see Cycles, 7-year).

Recession Cycle—A recurring period of 6-10 years (averaging 7 years in length), that defines the periodicity of recessions.

Safety—Low danger of default. One of three critical requirements for any investment during periods of massive economic and financial change.

Savings Bonds—Debt obligations of the U.S. government. Are sold at a discount from face value, and the bond's value rises every year, reflecting interest earned. At maturity, the bond returns full face value.

Sentinel Index—A proprietary index of Strayer Investment Advisers, Inc., that combines the many market indicators used into one number, to determine if one should be buying, selling, or holding common stocks, bonds, or gold stocks.

Short Sale—The act of borrowing shares and then selling them, with the objective of buying them back later at a lower price for return of shares to the lender. This is one of the few practical ways an investor can profit from declining share prices.

❖ *Glossary of Terms* ❖

Split, Stock—An adjustment in the number of outstanding shares by a corporation, without affecting changes in shareholder equity. In a 2-for-1 split, for example, you would suddenly own twice as many shares, each at half the price as before. (Practically speaking, it's like exchanging a $100 bill for two $50 bills.) As a general rule of thumb, corporations dislike their share prices to rise above $100 or decrease below $10, and use splits (or reverse splits) to influence investor attitudes about "expensive" or "cheap" stocks.

Superfund Account—An aggressive method for achieving distant goals, for those individuals with very limited investment funds or particularly challenging financial objectives.

Treasury Bills—Short-term debt obligations of the U.S. government, with maturities of one year or less. Treasury bills are sold at a discount from face value, and full repayment at maturity includes interest earned. Interest is exempt from state and local, but not federal, taxes. Typically considered one of the safest paper securities available.

Treasury Notes—Long-term debt obligations of the U.S. government, with maturities of 1 to 10 years. Interest is typically paid every six months. Interest is exempt from state and local, but not federal, taxes.

Treasury Bonds—Long-term debt obligations of the U.S. government, with maturities of 10 years or longer. Interest is typically paid every six months. Interest is exempt from state and local, but not federal, taxes.

Appendix

Recommended Investment Companies and Service Organizations:

Benham Group, The—A no-load mutual fund family that offers the securities felt to be most important over the next four years, and who ranks highest based on criteria offered in the book for choosing mutual funds. 1665 Charleston Road, Mountain view, CA 94043 1-800-4SAFETY (800-472-3389)

National Association of Investors Corporation—A group dedicated to assisting individuals in organizing and running investment clubs. 711 West Thirteen Mile Road, Madison Heights, MI 48071 810-583-6242

Scudder Funds—A no-load mutual fund family that offers the securities felt to be most important over the next four years, and who rank high based on the criteria offered in the book for choosing mutual funds. Two International Place, Boston, MA 02110 1-800-225-2470

Strayer Investment Advisers, Inc.—An independent investment advisory company that manages investment funds for clients and assists in financial planning and education. 7840 Madison Avenue, Suite 185, Fair Oaks, CA 95628 1-916-WORKING (916-967-5464)

Wall Street Journal, The—An excellent daily investment newspaper, recommended for investors who wish to refine their investment acumen. 200 Burnett Road, Chicopee, MA 01020 1-800-JOURNAL (800-568-7625)

Index

advance/decline 186
annuities 111, 215
antiques 111
Apollo Strategy 200
art 111
asset inflation 68
assets, non-monetary 89-90
assets work sheet 87-88
astrology 80
automobiles 128

balance sheet 86-88
bankers 33
banks:
 role in inflation/deflation 46, liquidity 47
Batra, Ravi 19, 72, 73
belief systems 27-39
Benham Group, The 191, 192, 194, 221, 222, 261
Bible, The 82, 247
bond indicators 188
bond funds:
 loaded 108, no-loads 108
bonds:
 corporate 108, 216, 50/60 year price cycles 173, 174, government agency 108, 216, municipal 108, 216,

7-year price cycles 75, 175, 177, treasury 107, 140-147, 216
books 34, 69
budget work sheet, target 122
business, your 112, 138, 219, 234, 235, starting one 230, valuation 87
business owners 77
business television 35-36

call date, bonds 140
cash, as king 71
cash expenses, how to record 99
cash flow 103
cash value, life insurance 214
Caterpillar, Inc. 7-8
certificates of deposit 106, 214
CPAs 32, 235-236
checking accounts 130
choices 120-122
COLAG 188
collectibles 111, 218
commercial paper 106
commodity futures 112, 116-117
consolidation, debt 130
consumer price index chart 53

conventional account 194, 199, 206, 221-223
coupon rate, bonds 140
"cows and bonds" 142
crash of 1929, cause 64
crash of 1987 188, cause 50
credit cards 90-91, 129
cycles 3, 59-84, 210, as investment tools 178, 181, charts 61, 75, 173, 175, deflation 60, 73, 172-174, 54 year repetition 62, 50/60 year 60, 73, 172-174, Kondratieff Wave chart 61, last long wave described 64-72, recession 74-78, 175-176, social 243

DEBT:
consolidation 130, corporate 16, government 17, personal 14-16, reasons 16
debt-free 202, 205
debtors 71
Deferred Compensation Plans 88, 220-221, 236
deflation 44, 65, 73, 177, defined 44, effect on debt payments 44, hedges 146, 152
deflation cycle 60, 172, bond prices 174, 177, causes 78, 83, gold prices 174, 177 stock prices 172, 176
denial 3, 12, 22
deposit guarantees, federal 48, 214
deposit insurance 47-48
diamonds 111, 218
discount rate 49

diversification 134
dividends, stock 136
dysfunctional companies 5
dysfunctional countries 9
dysfunctional families 4

education system 28
Elliott Wave 73
Employee Investment Plans 88, 219-221, 236
expense planning 125-128
expense work sheet 95-97
expenses recording 94, 98-99, non-monthly 99
expense review 101-102, 120-122
experience, as teacher 29
Exter, John 18

false prosperity 69, 172
FDIC 48, 214
federal funds rate 185, 188
Federal Reserve Board 74, influence on money supply 48, limited power 50, 50/60 year cycles (see deflation cycle)
financial assets inflation 69
financial objectives 198
financial planners 32
financial planning 197-207, 212, growth vs income 168
financial security 203, 205
financial serenity 200, 205
financially vulnerable 201, 205
FNMAs 108
formula, adjusting for inflation 54
found money 125, 128-132,

❖ *Index* ❖

226, 228
free reserves 185
FSLIC 48
futures, commodity 112, 116-117

gambler, professional 105, 182
generational effects on cycles 79
GICs 111, 215
gifting money to children 129
GNMAs 108
goal-setting 197-198
gold 110, 148-151, 218, as money 148, bullion coins 201, confiscation 150, 50/60 year price cycles 173-174, indicators 189, influences on price 150, its role 148, 7-year cycles 75, 175, 177
gold-backed currencies 149-150
gold mining stocks 148-155, 50/60 year price cycles 173-174, in a deflation 153-154, no-load funds 110, price leveraging 151-152, probable price changes 153, 177, production costs 151-152, 7-year price cycles 75, 175-176
government agency bonds 108, 216
guaranteed investment contracts (GICs) 111, 215
guarantees, federal deposit 48, 214

Homestake Mining 153, 154
hyperinflation 145, 172, 180

income, increasing it: employees 228-231, self-employed 234-235, income work sheet 93-94
indicators: stock 185, bond 198, gold mining stock 189, Sentinel Index 187
IRAs 219, magic of compounding 224-225
inflation 43, 76, 188, adjusting for 52, defined 43, effect on stock prices, example 55, 193, effect on real estate, example 42, highest recorded 57, myths 56
information sources 28-36, 210
insiders 139
insurance agents 31
insurance cash value 129, 214
interest rates 49, 74, 76 142-145, negative 145
inventory, financial 85-103
investment advisers 33
investment allocations by market 178-179
investment clubs 195, 213, 223-224, 226
investment psychology 181-183
investment strategy 178-179, 221-224, 235-239
investment timing 78, 182-185
investments, evaluation of 106-112, 210, chart 113
investments, non-monetary 120
investor categories 13

Japan, current role 72

Kondratieff Wave 60-63, 71

labor inflation 67
liabilities 90-91
liabilities work sheet 91-92
life insurance 31, 111, 215
liquidity 104, psychological liquidity 105
long-term investing 193, 237, stock example 55

magazines 35
managed accounts 212-213, 261
management review form 232-234
market competition 189
Mayans 62
minimum reserve requirement 46
monetary abuse 53, 149
money: defined 148, growth/supply 43-44, magic of compounding 224-225
money market funds 106, 214 explained 168-170, gov't only 107, 115
moving averages 188-189
mutual funds 190-195, 216-217, 221-223, choosing the best 191-192, how they work 166-168, no-load 166-168

National Association of Investers Corp. 213, 261
net capital 92-93

news, danger in making decisions 136-137, 139
newspapers 34
1920s, current similarities 63, 71-72
1929 74
1974, as turning point 68
1990, similarity to 1929 74
numerology 82

oil prices, influence on inflation 56
options 112, 115, 162-166, 185

par value, bonds 140
parental teaching 29
partnerships, limited 111, 217, 236
people-pleasing 133
Perot, H. Ross 18
planetary influences on cycles 79-81
politicians 29-30, 246
precious metals 110, 218
Prechter, Robert 73
primary recession 62
professional assistance 212-213, 261, 272
professional gambler 105, 182

real estate debt 64-65
real estate 42, 109, 155-162, 215, as choice of lifestyle 155, as investment 155-156, as a futures contract 159, decision factors 160-161, in a deflation 158-159, investment options 161
real growth potential 104

❖ Index ❖

recession cycle 73, 74-78, causes 78
recession cycle, effects on:
  stock prices 75, 174-176
  bond prices 75, 174-176
  gold prices 75, 174-176
  real estate prices 178
recession, primary 62
REITs 109, 168, 215
renters 203-204

safety 104
savings bonds 107, 218
Scudder Funds 192, 261
second mortgages 109, 215
Sentinel Index 187
"setup", the 14
7-year cycles (see recession cycle)
share rentals 130
shelter-secure 202, 205
short sales 137
silver 110, 218
Snyder, Julian M. 62
speculation 73
spending motivations 100-102
splits, stock 137
stamps 111, 218
stock indicators 185
stock market debt 65
stock mutual funds, loaded 110, no-loads 110
stockbrokers 31, 139
stocks 109, 135-139, 217, 7-year price cycles 75, 175-176, 50/60 year price cycles 172-174, probable price changes 176
stop losses, stock 217
Strayer Investment Advisers, Inc. 190, 213, 224, 261, 273
supercycles 73, grand supercycles 74
superfund 195-196, 199, 206, 223-224
survey, 100 of 100, 36

tax withholding 129
taxes 235-236
television, business 35-36
treasury bills 107, 188, 216
treasury bonds 107, 140-147, 216, 50/60 year price cycles 173-174, influences on price changes 142-145, no-load funds 108, probable price changes 147, 7-year price cycles 75, 175, 177
treasury note 107
trust deeds 109, 215

universal life insurance 111, 215

Wall Street Journal 242, 262
wars 65, as result of economics 62
"what everyone knows..." 36, 139

yield 140

zero coupon bonds 146-147

Author's Biography

THE FOLLOWING IS a biography of the author of *Debt-Free In Four Years*. Also included is information for contacting him.

Robert E. Strayer was born May 18, 1945, in Palisade, Nebraska, where he attended public school and played all sports. As a "straight-A" student he refused earlier offers to be advanced a grade, and graduated valedictorian.

Strayer developed his early business acumen from his father, Virgil Strayer, a businessman, entrepreneur, and Aksarben award-winner.

Enrolling at the University of Nebraska in 1963, he joined Triangle Fraternity, which accepts scientists, engineers, math majors, and architects. He spearheaded the fastest growth in that chapter's history, became its president, helped plan its new home, and was elected to the all-greek honorary, Gamma Gamma.

His exceptional grades earned him a scholarship and election to four honoraries. He became president of one honorary fraternity and was voted Outstanding Senior Student in his department by fellow classmates. In 1967 he was the third most recognized student at the large university. The only two students surpassing him were a member of his own fraternity, of which he was president, and the quarterback of the University of Nebraska football team.

At the height of the Vietnam War, he applied for Officer's

❖ *Debt-Free In Four Years* ❖

Training School, first with the Air Force and then the Navy. Strayer was eventually classified 1-Y, having broken his ankle four times playing basketball.

Upon receiving his Master's Degree, he accepted employment at the worldwide headquarters of Caterpillar, Inc., where he worked in marketing management for 12 years; received an outstanding management evaluation (the highest possible); and was featured in the company's worldwide service publication. Caterpillar is often referred to as one of the best-managed corporations in America, and in the 1970s was also our country's largest export earner. Strayer designed a strategy for integrating prime product, parts, and service sales, which is still in use today. His last function with this huge Fortune Fifty company was preparing their first worldwide service marketing plan.

He received considerable international business experience while traveling in 29 different countries, and living and working 6 years in Geneva, Switzerland; Paris, France; and Johannesburg, South Africa. He quickly learned French and conducted business in that language for 2 1/2 years. During this overseas period he conducted operations studies, consulted management, evaluated the economic, political, and social trends of several countries, determined how client companies were reacting to sales opportunities, and either adapted or developed programs to help these companies increase their business.

In 1977 he began studying the works of James Dines, one of the world's four most successful and longest-practicing investment advisers. Dines had been the leader in urging a gold standard and the purchase of precious metals. It was not known at the time that if Dines told everyone when to buy, it would be Strayer himself that would issue the best gold stock sell signal in the business in the fall of 1980, within two weeks of their all-time high. Mr. Dines became a subscriber to Mr. Strayer's newsletter.

During his last four years with Caterpillar, Strayer's stock investments yielded an annualized 112% return on invest-

❖ *Author's Biography* ❖

ment. In 1980 he completed his state exams, and became a fully-registered investment adviser with the Securities and Exchange Commission in Washington, D.C. Mr. Strayer clearly stated in his registration that he would *never sell commissioned securities, insurance, or real estate*. As President of Strayer Investment Advisers, Inc., this has allowed him to clearly see economic and financial developments by removing vested interests from his observations. The company also *refuses to accept custody or possession of client funds*.

Since 1980, he has assisted numerous clients on financial matters from virtually every category: Salaried employees, hourly workers, U.S./overseas business owners, financial planners, CPAs, stockbrokers, bankers, economists, and even Nobel prize-winners.

Combined with his extensive worldwide experience, Strayer's research has produced a keen understanding of investment cycles and their profitable application. He has proven economic, social, and health trends move *in tandem*, in a precise and predictable manner. Strayer developed a proprietary set of indicators for the purchase and sale of common stocks, bonds, and gold mining stocks. The success of such tools were not only proven for gold stocks in 1980, but prior to the October, 87 stock market crash. Strayer moved clients totally out of stocks two weeks before Black Monday, avoiding a 35% plunge in prices.

An award-winning speaker, he has been aired several times on TV and radio, and has won numerous speech contests with Toastmasters International. He has served as Governor and District Governor for TI, and in 1994 served as club president of the 3rd-rated toastmasters club in the world (among 7,000 clubs).

Strayer has gained widespread recognition and become a popular speaker in business, professional, and college circles. His articles on investing and political, economic, and social change have appeared in various Illinois and California newspapers. He wrote and published his own monthly investment newsletter for seven years.

❖ *Debt-Free In Four Years* ❖

His first book, *Debt-Free In Four Years*, was originally printed locally in Sacramento, CA within four weeks of the exact peak of the California economic cycle in 1990 under the title *Forgive Us Our Debts...*, and accurately predicted economic, market, and business trends now being experienced. While most people are confused by current events, readers not only understood what is happening, but how and why, and exactly what to do about it. The next four years are critical to one's finances, and will result in massive profits or financial ruin, depending on one's investment choices and how fast debt is eliminated.

Strayer's second book, *Tears of Sorrow...Tears of Joy* will soon be published (subject to title change by publisher, Clayton House). This work will complete an original trilogy on financial serenity, self-development, and spiritual growth. (The first section was printed as a book early due to imminent financial change, and the fact that people fighting financial problems cannot focus clearly on personal development.) When used together, the two books provide a precise and effective path for protecting and growing one's assets, eliminating greed and financial fears, applying true psychotherapy, and allowing individuals to remember who they are and why they are here.

Both books are immediately available electronically via modem, (916) 962-3467.

Readers may contact the author:

Robert E. Strayer
Strayer Investment Advisers, Inc.,
7840 Madison Avenue, Suite 185
Fair Oaks, CA 95628-3518
916-WORKING (916-967-5464).

Data: (916) 962-3467
User Name: STRAYER

Internet Mail: WL-STRAYER-FB@SOCIETY.COM
(Internet address subject to change without notice due to Internet expansion.)